Dorset Smugglers

First published in 2016 by Natula Publications,
5 St Margaret's Avenue, Christchurch, Dorset BH23 1JD

ISBN 9781897887486

A CIP catalogue record of this book is available from the British Library.

Printed in England

Contents

Acknowledgements

I would like to thank all the people who helped me to make this book possible. I also wish to thank all those who have provided me with information and material: the, *Bournemouth Evening Echo,* the staff at the Red House Museum & Gardens Heritage Museum and the staff at the Dorset History Centre and the aerial photos by Shamus Pitts, Wessex Hang Gliding and Paragliding Club, Neville Almond, Sky Surfing and Hang Gliding Club. I wish to thank my wife, Chrys and Trevor Humphrey, for the many reads and re-reads of the text.

Introduction

Firstly, I would like to pose a question I want you to consider: was smuggling an exciting and romantic profession as it has been depicted, or was it a hard life beset by dangers on every side? Hopefully this book will help you answer that question. There are many extracts from the Poole, Weymouth and Cowes Letter Books (customs records) and a raft of eyewitness accounts from reporters working for the *Salisbury and Winchester Journal.* I even found references in the parliamentary records.

I have delved into many reference books to gather information and data for this work, and the journey I have taken whilst researching and writing has been one of remarkable discovery. I hope the chilling stories of the smugglers and revenue men contained herein illustrate what a fascinating subject it really is.

The Dorset coastline of 200–300 years ago was as beautiful as it is today; however, it was not always as safe for the seafaring community. Seamen lived and worked up and down the coast, but were perpetually forced to hide from the Impress Service – those men who tried to force any able-bodied young man into His Majesty's Royal Navy. Smugglers were ideal candidates, good hardy seamen used to hard work and life on the high seas. Still at least the navy were legitimate; it would have been much worse to get caught up with the smugglers who worked and roamed the coast. It was a treacherous life and if you were unlucky enough to be caught smuggling by the revenue officers, then you were likely to end up in Dorchester Gaol, not a place you would really want to be. If you could not afford to pay the fine you were left to rot until either, you found the money, or the authorities decided to release you. Worse still, if you obstructed the revenue officers in their line of duty, or struck an officer in his line of duty, then you were sentenced to hard labour. Often prisoners were 'encouraged' by the Impress Service into joining the navy; for many smugglers this was one of the worst fates imaginable and was greatly feared. Of course, there were those who met their Maker at the end of a rope, as was the case with the leaders of the Hawkhurst gang, who were hanged for murder – and a gruesome murder it was too. However, you didn't have to be caught with your hands on contraband to suffer the consequences; if you were caught signalling a smuggling vessel out at sea you could end up being transported to one of Britain's overseas plantations – most likely in the Americas.

All along the Dorset coast there were many battles between the revenue men and the smugglers. The tranquil beaches often ran red with blood, as happened at the Haven at Mudeford in 1784. Today it is a beautiful resort, frequented by holidaymakers and locals who often take their children crabbing in the waters around the Haven, as I once did as a child. There is also the wonderful Haven Inn (not the original inn) where you can sit outside and have a quiet drink and watch the world go by.

In Chapters 3 and 4, I have taken the individual cases of the most infamous smugglers and the most officious revenue men, to show both sides of the story.

So, at this point I leave it to you, the reader, to make up your minds. Was smuggling a romantic profession or was it an unscrupulous and hard life of sin? I know what I believe the answer to that question should be. What do you think?

1

Smuggling: How it started and developed

In the famous dictionary of 1765 by Dr Johnson, he describes a smuggler as, 'A wretch who in defiance of justice and laws imports or exports goods either contraband or without payment of the customs.'

Adam Smith, the great eighteenth-century economist and advocate of free trade wrote, 'A smuggler is a person who, though no doubt blameable for violating the laws of his country, is frequently incapable of violating those of natural justice, and would have been in every respect an excellent citizen had not the laws of his country made that a crime which nature never meant to be so.'[1]

The origins of serious smuggling lie in the steep increases in taxes that came about in the eighteenth century as Parliament struggled to finance Britain's expansionist policy of empire building. Between 1775 and 1815, British forces were involved in three major wars: the, American War of Independence (1775–1783); the War of Jenkins' War with Spain (1739–1748); and the Napoleonic Wars (1793–1815). Add to this an ever-increasing demand for naval advancement and it is clear to see why the British authorities had little option but to take an aggressive stance to raising taxes.

Parliament raised funds to fight these wars by introducing a tax, or duty, on commodities entering and leaving the country. A book of rates was introduced, which listed all of the items on which duty would be paid when imported or exported. The book of rates was constantly updated with new items, and the taxes or duty paid for those already listed was usually increased to meet financial demands on the state.

It all started in 1275 when King Edward I, looking for a new way to raise revenue, introduced a tax on the export of wool out of the Port of London and thirteen other ports around the country. It was at this point that the smuggling trade was truly born. The first active smugglers were known as 'Owlers', a name most likely derived from their nocturnal activities. At the same time, Collectors of Customs

---

[1] Quoted in *The Life of Adam Smith* by Ian Simpson Ross.

were appointed by Royal Patent as a method of collecting this new form of revenue. A temporary Board of Customs was created by ordinance on 21 January 1643 and from then on the regulation of the collection of customs was passed to a parliamentary committee. This continued until 1660 when the Crown took over, which lasted until 1671. However, this situation was untenable and so a permanent Board of Customs was established, which saw the appointment of six commissioners to manage customs' duties in England and Wales.

Law's introduced by Edward I dictated that wool could only be exported via certain ports, which were named the staple ports. Poole became a staple port in 1433, but this did not stop the smuggling in Dorset. The smugglers found many quiet and secluded spots along the coast where they could load and unload their vessels without being disturbed. The area the customs men had to cover was extremely large and patrolling them was effectively impossible, affording the smugglers every chance of avoiding detection.

William Lowe, a customs officer in the mid-fifteenth century, was typical of his breed. His area of influence covered Dorset from the border with Devon eastwards along the coast to Hampshire and into Sussex. His only mode of transport was his trusted horse, but he was a highly dedicated officer and earned the reputation for being highly conscientious and an officer of integrity. In his time as a revenue officer William Lowe seized many cargoes of wool and leather, and as such the merchants and smugglers came to loathe him. In 1452, he seized a Dutch ship loaded high with goods that fifteen merchants from Sherborne, Bridport and Charminster were trying to smuggle out of the country. In the year that followed the seizure, William Lowe was attacked by a London wool merchant who, according to Lowe, 'smote me with a dagger in the nose, and through the nose into the mouth'. Luckily for William he survived the attack and lived to write a full report of the incident.

During the reign of Henry VII the customs service gradually improved. This encouraged growth in the levels of foreign trade and consequently the levels of duty available in 1507. This increase in taxes collected helped boost the coffers of the treasury.

In the sixteenth century, around 1558, Queen Mary's government revised the book of rates[2]. This saw a slow rise in smuggling and its progression from being a part-time activity to an illegal profession. Smuggling became more of a two-way street with the import and export of illegal goods. There was no improvement in the collection of duties, but there was an increase in the amount of bribery and corruption involving government officials. Many 'favours' were accepted to obtain permits and licences. It was not unusual for officials to show a blind eye and, as the saying goes, to 'cross the palm with silver'.

During the reign of Elizabeth I, the authorities began to realise the scale of the losses to revenue incurred by the government due to the smugglers, not forgetting the proliferation of corruption within the custom service which was causing a major loss in potential revenue. Preventative steps were taken in 1564 when each of the smaller ports was given record books. This parchment book, or 'Port Book', had numbered pages and a cord held in place with the exchequer's seal, for verification. There were two separate books: one for overseas vessels and one for coastal vessels. They recorded details of the following: the vessels' tonnage, their home port, who the master was and their destination or next port, as well as the cock'ets (receipts) showing details of any duty paid. On many occasions false information would have been supplied, such as their proposed destination. Before 1600 the entries would have been in Latin. It wasn't until 1660 that they started to appear in English.

However, this corruption was not restricted to the customs officials; Members of Parliament and foreign officials were involved too. They were allowed to import goods duty free for their own consumption, but like most honour systems this was widely abused. In reality, a lot of these people were either in league with the smugglers, or knew of their actions. For example, the Bishop of Exeter sometimes imported far more than he would himself use; these goods would have been ordered by his steward in the bishop's name and who knows what he did with the excess. Members of Parliament and foreign ambassadors all had similar privileges and no doubt they would have abused the system also.

---

[2] For example, in 1550 French wine was 3*s* 4*d* per ton and after the increase in taxes of 1558, the price for French wine was 53*s* 4*d* per ton.

In 1643, at the time of the Civil War, to meet the cost of the warfare, there was another increase in taxes. It was supposedly only a temporary amendment, but the changes stayed. However, in this case the duty was to be paid by the buyer, similar to the modern VAT structure and, initially, it applied to beer, cider, perry and strong waters. However, as ever, further items were added to the list including chocolate, sherbet, coffee and tea.

Despite increased vigilance, combating the smugglers did not improve as the years passed. If we look at Poole on 11 August 1764, the collector wrote about the extent of smuggling within the area and the types of goods being smuggled which included tea, raw coffee, tobacco, tobacco stakes, brandy, rum, gineva (gin) and currants.

A report, dated 31 October 1783, showed continued increase in smuggling within the Christchurch and Poole area. The report detailed the propagation of smuggling over the previous three years and concluded that additional officers would not be sufficient to curtail the smugglers' activities. It recommended the creation of a proper force at sea and a military presence on land, large enough to suppress the smuggling trade along the coast.

Another report twenty years later, dated 31 December 1804, once more gives a detailed report of the smuggling within the area, and goes on to list the quantities arriving and how the goods were brought in and distributed. Many of the goods that were run into Christchurch and Poole would have been taken into the New Forest, been hidden away and then from there distributed throughout Hampshire and Wiltshire. These included spirituous liquors, wine, tobacco and salt from Guernsey and Jersey.

One might assume that goods entering this area would have ended up in the London area, but this was not the case. Goods landed within the Purbecks would have been sent to Bristol, Bath and Trowbridge, or other manufacturing areas, and then dispersed in smaller quantities.

Smuggling had become big business, in fact, a very serious business, involving people from all walks of life, all driven by the same desire – to make money. The smugglers or 'free traders', as they liked to be known, believed that they were driven to this end by the actions of the monarchs and governments of the time.

There were many reports sent to the authorities on the levels of smuggling within Dorset and surrounding areas, with a copy even reaching the Prime Minister of the day, Lord Shelburne. The Commissioner of Customs detailed the estimated number of people involved, the number of wagons and horses deployed in the trade and even how far afield the contraband travelled into the industrial areas of the country – Oxfordshire, Worcestershire and Warwickshire.

The laws against smuggling were being updated constantly (*see* Chapter 6). Calls for reform and changes were sent to the Home Secretary, as we can see from a William Pitt, who reported back to the Home Secretary on the amount of revenue lost to the smugglers over a ten-year period.

In 1766, the duty paid was £1,114,677 12*s* ¼*d.* But by 1776, the duty paid was £1,060,391 5*s* 6*d.*

A substantial reduction in revenue collected, considering the amount of tea consumed throughout the country had increased, along with the population; it does not take much to see the correlation between smuggling and the decrease in revenue collected.

Another option opens to the smugglers, during times of war, was to turn to privateering along with the revenue cutters. With the outbreak of war with France in 1793, the government took no time in granting ship owners with a letter of Marque, or licence. This allowed the ship owners to attack and seize French merchant ships and their cargoes in the name of the King; in reality this was a legalised form of piracy, authorised by the British government. However, the merchants themselves had to be careful as France also had their own privateers. They too could be captured and taken back to France as prisoners along with their vessels and goods.

Privateering was a potentially lucrative pastime and as such many vessels were purchased and converted into warships, armed and made ready to take on the enemy. In times of war this was a way of mobilising a fleet of warships without committing any public money. The vessels would have been overmanned, ready to crew the vessels they hoped to capture and bring home

Reading through the Cowes and Poole Letter Book, I came across many vessels that had been granted such a letter of Marque. One was the *Swan*, a revenue cutter based in Cowes, captained by a Francis Sarman. There was also the *Dover*, a 66-ton lugger, with a crew of forty men under the command of John Matthews; its letter of Marque was granted 11 April 1793 and a member of its crew was a young John Rattenbury, a smuggler from the West Country.

'Letters of Marque' worked quite easily. The ship had to provide the following information before being granted the licence: its name, tonnage, firepower, number of its crew and the name of its captain. The captain was also expected to perform the following:

> [To] keep an exact journal of his proceedings, and therein particularly to take notice of all prizes which shall be taken by him, the nature of such prizes, the time and place of their being taken, the value of them as near as he can judge, as also the situation, motion and strength of the French, as well as he can discover by the best intelligence he can get; of which he is, from time to time as he shall have opportunity, to transmit an account to our secretary.[3]

The types of items that smugglers imported would often have been purchased honestly, with either the smuggler's own money or money from a benefactor. This is one of the reasons why it was such a precarious profession. If a smuggler had bought 3 tonnes of rum on the understanding that he would receive cash on delivery upon his return, only for his cargo to be taken by customs or to be lost at sea, then he could be ruined. Though, on some occasions, often to eliminate the possibility of anyone talking to the revenue officers, the financing was spread throughout the community. With everyone having a share in the cargo, there was much less chance that someone would snitch.

It also appears that the suppliers of the contraband in France and the Netherlands had a direct hand in the importation of illegal spirits to Britain. They would load their own vessels with the goods and rendezvous with smaller vessels from Britain who would then purchase the goods at sea before smuggling them into the country. This was a much safer route to market for British smugglers but they were then at the mercy of the Europeans when it came to price.

Smugglers did not see themselves as criminals, and rather thought of themselves as 'free traders', performing a public service by giving people access to goods that in reality they would never have been able

---

[3] Pro ADM7/328.

to afford. This belief was evident when smugglers had a cargo taken by the authorities. They were willing to try to retrieve it by any means as Isaac Gulliver did in 1778 when he seized back a cargo from the supervisor's house in Blandford uttering the words, 'So we shall be taking what is ours thank you sir.' Even the gentry themselves would benefit from the smugglers actions and some financially supported the purchase and transportation of the cargoes. Indeed, it was not unheard of for some smugglers to have their fines paid by their rich benefactors.

The type of cargo transported would vary greatly depending on the recipients and the season. Goods smuggled between 1700 and 1850 along the South of England included, as well as spirits, silk and tobacco, playing cards, logwood, beverages, dried fruit, perfume and British gold sovereigns[4]. These coins could be sold for 30*s*, making a profit of 50 per cent. It is said that gold coins like this, to the value of £10,000 per week, were smuggled out and sold, and much of the finances generated for the war with France was raised in London.

The smugglers did not confine themselves to carrying the items listed above; during times of war, for example, letters and newspapers were carried across the Channel to France. Also, during wartime, spies and nobility served as valuable cargo to be shipped across the Channel and during the wars with France, escaped French prisoners of war would have been smuggled back, an early version of people trafficking.

Smuggling did tend to appeal to the worst segments of society, and as such the trade attracted lawbreakers and ruthless villains, who thought nothing of shooting to kill or using extreme violence to protect their interests.

One such ruthless gang of smugglers was the Hawkhurst gang from Kent. They made a visit to Poole one evening, and broke into the custom house to retrieve a cargo of tea which had been seized. As they removed their ill-gotten goods they said, 'We come for our own and we will have it'. As a result of these kinds of break-ins, running battles between the revenue men and the smugglers often occurred, normally ending with somebody being killed or seriously injured, turning quiet, tranquil beaches into battlefields running red with blood.

---

[4] For a more detailed list please see the Appendix

However, it seems that the smugglers did command a certain amount of respect in the local community. This may have been due to fear of reprisals or from simple admiration for what the smugglers were doing. If they needed a helping hand to move a cargo, then the villagers would rally around and a gang of 200-plus strong could be gathered very quickly to assist in the landing and running of a consignment.

There is a story of a milkmaid who walked around the village with two buckets of milk and each had a particular number of wooden balls, depending on where and when the contraband was to be landed. A farm labourer could earn more money as a tub man than working on the farm, so for many families this would have been a good way to make ends meet. In fact, the profits that could be made were so high that the smugglers could lose one in three of their cargoes and still be able to make a profit.

The government also discouraged the purchase and sale of foreign goods by means of 'Protectionism'. This protected local business and encouraged people to use items made in the country over those items which were imported. Officials believed that by imposing a heavy import duty on goods entering the country and thus making them very expensive to purchase that it would lead to home production of the same items and further protection of the home market.

2

Smugglers of Dorset

Isaac Gulliver
(Photo kindly supplied courtesy of Bournemouth Evening Echo)

Isaac Gulliver (1745–1822)

Isaac Gulliver was born in the Wiltshire village of Semington on 5 September 1745, to Isaac and Elizabeth Gulifor. He was baptised on the same day in the local church, not far from Trowbridge. Being born in Semington meant that he was a true Wiltshire Moonraker.

Isaac Gulliver was to become a legend in his own time. He was charming and yet mysterious, and one of the most notorious and successful smugglers of his time. Gulliver and his gang of Moonrakers worked the Dorset and Hampshire coast from Christchurch, then in

Hampshire, westwards to Lyme Regis on the Dorset/Devon border running large quantities of illegal goods into the country from across the channel. Like so many others, they were depriving the government of the duty on the goods and, most importantly, supplementing their meagre wages. An interesting analogy of this would be that Gulliver was a 'Robin Hood' of his time, robbing the rich to feed the poor.

Little is known of Gulliver's early life, though it appears likely that he learned the smuggling trade from his father. A report in 1758 from the *Salisbury and Winchester Journal* mentions an incident involving an 'Isaac Gulliver' fighting with a customs officer, but at the time Gulliver would only have been twelve, so more than likely this would have been his father.

At the age of twenty-three, Gulliver married Elizabeth Beale, the daughter of William Beale, the tenant of a small alehouse, the Blacksmith Arms, in the small village of Thorney Down. The marriage took place on 5 October 1768 in the church of St Mary the Virgin in Six Penny Handley and was presided over by Philip Ridout.

Gulliver took over the tenancy of the inn, changing the name to the Kings Arms. He also fathered two daughters, Elizabeth and Ann, both of whom were baptised in the local church in 1770 and 1773 respectively. In 1774 he had a son and as the tradition he was named Isaac after his father. It appears that within this year, 1774, Gulliver, along with William Beale and Roger Ridout, had made his first entry in the Poole Letter Book.

By 1777 Gulliver was financially secure, either by inheritance from his father, or by other means, perhaps smuggling. He rented 75 acres of land and a malthouse at Kinson, but at the same time lent £300 and a 4.5 per cent mortgage to a farmer at Melbury Abbas.

During his time as a publican he amassed a large range of properties; he bought land at Ensbury and Cudnell, along with properties in Kinson. He also managed to acquire Pitts Farm in Kinson (one of his first major expenditures). Many of these estates were in special places and bought for specific reasons. For example, in 1776 Gulliver purchased North Eggardon Farm from William Chaffin after his brother, George Chaffin, died. The farm lay 6 miles from the coast and the property boasted Eggardon Hill, one the highest points in Dorset. The coastline is visible to the south from this hilltop and all approaches to the hill can be clearly seen. It is feasible that this property was purchased purely for this vantage point. It would have allowed anyone to see the arrival of any vessel and thus enabled the smugglers on the shore to signal to the ships when it was safe for them to land their valuable cargoes.

As the years passed Gulliver managed to accumulate a vast network of vaults, hiding places where goods could be moved on easily and safely without detection. These places were along the Dorset coastline and inland along the routes taken by the smugglers. Gulliver also seems to have gathered a fleet of ships ranging from 20–70 tons, all capable of carrying contraband from France to the English coast.

Gulliver and his followers gained a reputation, becoming known as the White Wigs, due to the fact that they grew their hair long and then sprinkled white powder into it, echoing the fashion of the bourgeoisie of the day. This was a dig at the gentry because the expense of powder meant that it would only have been worn on special occasions.

In the spring of 1778 a number of revenue men from Blandford came into Thorney Down and seized nine casks of liquor and over ¾ of a ton of tea from right under Gulliver's nose. His reaction was to gather up his men and go into Blandford to retrieve the goods. Armed with blades, clubs and pistols they mounted their horses and made their way to the supervisor's house. They also took along a horse and wagon to carry away the casks of liquor and the tea. Led by Gulliver with Roger Ridout at his side (whom Isaac brought because he knew the way to the supervisor's house) they travelled through the streets of Blandford until they reached the house. They stopped and gathered around the front of it.

As a crowd of onlookers from the local inn cheered him on, Gulliver leant down from his horse and knocked on the front door. No sound came from inside the house. Gulliver, ever the showman, announced to the onlookers, 'So we shall be taking what is ours thank you sir.'

His men dismounted and they called upon Joseph the blacksmith to force open the door. Quickly they entered the building looking for their property, located and loaded it up the wagon with great efficiency and speed. As the last man came out a cheer rose from the crowd. The smugglers left the onlookers with two barrels before making their way home. As they clattered their way down through the cobbled streets, they fired off their pistols whilst the crowd behind them gathered around the two casks of brandy they had been gifted.

In 1777 a foolish man by the name of Levi Payne stole Gulliver's year old grey horse and £21 6*s* which he had collected on the smuggler's behalf. Gulliver advertised and offered a reward for the return of his property, but who knows what really happened to Levi – the network of smugglers would have easily seen him riding such a distinctive horse …

Gulliver acquired the White Hart in Longham in 1779. This building still stands and is still as popular today. Once again it appears the inn was chosen for its location, not far from one of his many hiding places: St Andrew's Church at Kinson. It is from this inn that Gulliver advertised the sale of twenty good packhorses in the *Salisbury and Winchester Journal* on 29 March 1779.

St Andrews Church in Kinson still bears the scars of the smuggling days. They would haul the contraband up the outside of the tower and into the church. If you look inside the church, you can see how the ropes cut into the stonework of the archway as they lifted the kegs and cargo up and down the tower. Their methods were quite ingenious: they would throw a rope over the parapet of the tower, between the castellation, and drop it down inside the tower. Then it was all hands to the fore as they hauled the rope down the centre aisle of the nave and the kegs up the outside of the church into the tower. Over the years the rope cut into the apex of the archway. It must have been an interesting spectacle to see kegs of spirits racing up and down the outside of the tower at night. But the smugglers did not want an audience. To keep people away from their activities they would invent stories of places being haunted and even go so far as to act out such hauntings. One involved dressing a young girl all in white, putting a false head under her arm and then placing her by the churchyard gates. If anybody approached she would moan and groan; that was enough to frighten even the most bold away. St Andrews Church is no different – there are many stories of the churchyard being haunted.

Gulliver's name features regularly in the Poole Letter Book and official letters. His next mention appears in 1780, after 541 gallons of brandy and rum, and 1,871lb of tea were seized from a John Singer of Kinson. Singer was reputed to be a servant of Isaac Gulliver.

In 1782 Gulliver's name turns up again, this time on a customs list for unshipping four pipes of wine without payment of duty. But once again Gulliver's luck was with him as the revenue officers who had been chasing the smuggler for many years again failed to get their man. There appears to be two stories on how he avoided being prosecuted and both could be true, but the first one I believe is more likely. Under the 1782 Act of Oblivion a smuggler could clear his name by serving in the Royal Navy. This was similar to the Smuggling Act of 1736, except that under this Act, Gulliver needed to find two people willing to take his place: one fit and able seaman and one fit and able land man. If he succeeded, then he would have been allowed to go free. Now, with the wealth that Gulliver had amassed this would not have been too hard a task for him to fulfil, despite only being given forty-four days to do so, and it appears that he was successful as he met the terms of the pardon.

The second, and less likely, story claims Gulliver foiled an attempt on the life of the King George III. He purportedly uncovered a plot against the king and as a reward for his loyalty the King said, 'Let Gulliver smuggle as much as he likes.'

In August of the same year Gulliver decided to move lock, stock, and barrel to Devon, and his shop in Kinson was to be let. He advertised in the *Salisbury and Winchester Journal* stating that he was moving to Teignmouth in Devonshire. But this was a ruse; instead of moving to Devon he bought Hillamsland Farm only 1 mile away in the parish of Hampreston, and in 1783 he was still trading as a wine merchant from Kinson.

The old house still stands today and can be found off the Christchurch Road. It is the old farmhouse adjoining the Dudsbury Golf course and unsurprisingly the house is reputedly haunted. Yet another story put out by the smugglers to keep people away, and the rumour persists to this day. But what were they trying to hide? The farmhouse has a sizable cellar, with signs of bricked-up entrances, but what lies behind them, and if they are passages where do they come out?

Gulliver's next encounter with the revenue men came in 1788, four years after an encounter with the crew of the customs cutter, the *Laural*. A party of about forty customs men lead by William Sander, the commander of the *Laural*, came face to face with a gang of 100 or more smugglers. The revenue men lost the battle before they could carry out any searches or seizures and retired to lick their wounds and regroup ready for the next time.

The White Hart at Longham

Gulliver's Farm in West Moors

Highe House, Corfe Mullen

No. 45 West Borough in Wimborne

The blue plaque on the wall at No. 45 West Borough in Wimborne

In 1788 a report from the Port of Poole shows that Gulliver was confining his activities to the wine trade (understandable considering he was a wine merchant) and selling wine at a considerably reduced rate. One wonders if he was selling off his vast stocks hidden away in the many cellars and hiding places along the coast? The report also mentions that Gulliver had retired and was living on a farm in the area.

At this stage Gulliver was forty-three and may well have reduced his smuggling activities, but had not given up entirely. He also sold off one of his properties. This may well have been Kinson Farm; the tenant was a Mr Tait, who was credited with the construction of Pelham House on the land in 1793, which was to become the residence of his eldest daughter, Elizabeth.

However, 1789 saw Gulliver add another property to his portfolio: Gulliver's Farm in West Moors, which is still in existence. At the time this would have been a remote place; sitting on the heath, it was a perfect place for a smuggler to hide contraband, and once again it was probably selected for its location being on the road to Cranborne the continuation of which leads you to Tippet crossroads and Thorney

Down. Whilst reading *In Search of Isaac Gulliver: Legendary Dorset Smuggler* by M.V. Angel, I came across another interesting fact to do with the road leading to the farm. It appears that there were bolt-holes along this road where smugglers could hide if being chased by revenue officers. These were still visible until the 1920s, but sadly no more. Gulliver's next venture appears to be the building of another vessel – a fast sleek ship, built for the sole purpose of smuggling and evading the revenue men. It was built by master craftsman Samuel Starling, and was dubbed the *Dolphin.* She was used to carry goods across the channel from France to the South Coast. The story of how Gulliver once more evaded the authorities starts with a trip from France to Bourne Heath aboard the *Dolphin.* Whilst landing the cargo he got wind of the pending arrival of the revenue men, in particular a Mr Weston, the Comptroller from Poole. However, the savvy Gulliver escaped by supposedly faking his own death. He lay in a coffin in state with his face white and ghostly – he had covered it with his old favourite, white powder. Apparently, to add some credence to the claim that he was dead, Gulliver added stones to the coffin for weight and had it interred.

The coffin was buried at East Howe Lodge, yet another of Gulliver's properties. When it was demolished in 1958, all of the hiding places used by the smuggler were uncovered; there was a trapdoor in the living room which led to a warren of tunnels leading off to the neighbouring property, the Red House (known as Ridouts House). What neighbours Roger Ridout and Isaac Gulliver would have made! Another secret passageway led into the chimney breast and came out into a large chamber about 4ft wide; whilst in the ceiling there was a trapdoor into the loft from which one could get back down between the vinery and the kitchen to the wood store and the stables – escape routes for when the revenue men came calling.

Interestingly, although the building was long-gone, it was still giving up its secrets in the 1980s; a stash of brandy bottles and some French pottery was found during an excavation of the site. And it was not just the odd bottle or two, there were thousands of them.

Then there is Highe House (a Grade II listed building) at Corfe Mullen, sitting on the corner of Wimborne Road and Candy Lane, with its distinctive green-tiled roof. If you look at the property from the front you can see what was once the Georgian coach house to the left, while on the right one can see what was once a single-storey cob cottage, but it has since been modified and a second storey added. This property was most likely purchased by Gulliver for its location; the clear views of the only road access and across the local countryside afforded the smuggler ample time to warn of any impending visits by the revenue officers or the town's red-coated dragoons. As was the case with the others of Gulliver's properties, there were legends and stories of underground tunnels and hiding places, but these are probably only stories as I do not believe any tunnels have been found, only a pit of broken clay pipes when new foundations were being excavated. Of course, there are the ghost stories: previous owners of the house and also the present owners have heard the sound of footsteps on the stairs and in the rooms upstairs when no one is there, and the smell of pipe tobacco pervades the air without source. But who is this smoking phantom? Could they be the footsteps of Isaac Gulliver himself?

Despite his commercial success, Gulliver was not immune to family problems. In 1797, after one year of marriage, his daughter, Ann, left her husband Edmund Wagg and fled, with the help of her brother, Isaac, taking all the linen and plates. Why they split is unknown, however, their differences must have been resolved quickly because she was back living with Wagg within the year. A year later the family was struck by tragedy; Gulliver's son, Isaac, died at the age of twenty-four and was duly buried in Wimborne Minster. Edmund Wagg, Ann's husband, died not long after her brother in 1799, and he too was buried in Wimborne Minster, under the specific request that he be interred in the same vault as his brother-in-law, Isaac Gulliver junior. Ann would later marry Dr William Fryer, a local physician and banker from the famed Fryer banking family.

A turning point in Gulliver's smuggling career came in 1800 when he landed his final cargo at Bournemouth: three large luggers laden to the gunnels with brandy, silk, tobacco and other valuable items. The story goes that when landed and loaded onto the horses and wagons the cortège stretched for around 2 miles with Gulliver at the front on his mount. The run, as usual, was a success.

The most incredible and intriguing fact about Isaac Gulliver is that in all his years as a smuggler he was never caught. He came close once or twice, but always managed to frustrate the revenue men by receiving a pardon – luck was ever on his side. In reading through many articles and books on Isaac Gulliver I find that I admire him; he was a born leader and knew how to motivate his men, how to get the best from them and how to keep their loyalty, as evidenced by his followers, the White Wigs.

In the latter part of his life Gulliver continued to move about the Dorset area: from 1793 to 1807 it appears that he stayed in residence at Long Crichel, only to move back to Kinson House in 1815. In 1816 Gulliver was still in residence at there when his daughter Elizabeth Fryer moved into Pelhams in Kinson with her husband, William. In 1817, Gulliver made his final move to No. 45 West Borough in Wimborne.

By now, Gulliver was a highly respected and wealthy man. On 13 September 1822, at the age of seventy-six, Gulliver died, leaving a 12,000-word will and an estate to the value of £60,000 – a vast fortune for the day. He was buried in Wimborne Minster. Over the years the public walking over his stone has made reading the inscription difficult, so to preserve it the stone was moved and mounted on the wall.

Upon his death, Gulliver made provisions for his wife by placing all his property throughout the counties of Dorset, Hampshire, Somerset and Wiltshire in trust to two local clergymen, and from the proceeds a sum of £400 per year was to be paid to his wife, Elizabeth. He also looked after his youngest daughter, Ann, who received a sum which in the end rose to £500 per annum. Not leaving the grandchildren out, a sum of £22,000 was to be divided between them – his seven grandsons were each to receive a share of two properties and £4,000 – whilst the remainder of the property was to go to his eldest daughter, Elizabeth. He may not have obeyed the laws of the land, but he was well-liked, even loved, and one of his main claims to fame was that no one died as the result of his activities. So who says smuggling does not pay – in Isaac Gulliver's case it certainly did!

St Andrews Church, Kinson

The Stocks Inn at Furzehill Wimborne

The Stocks Inn at Furzehill Wimborne

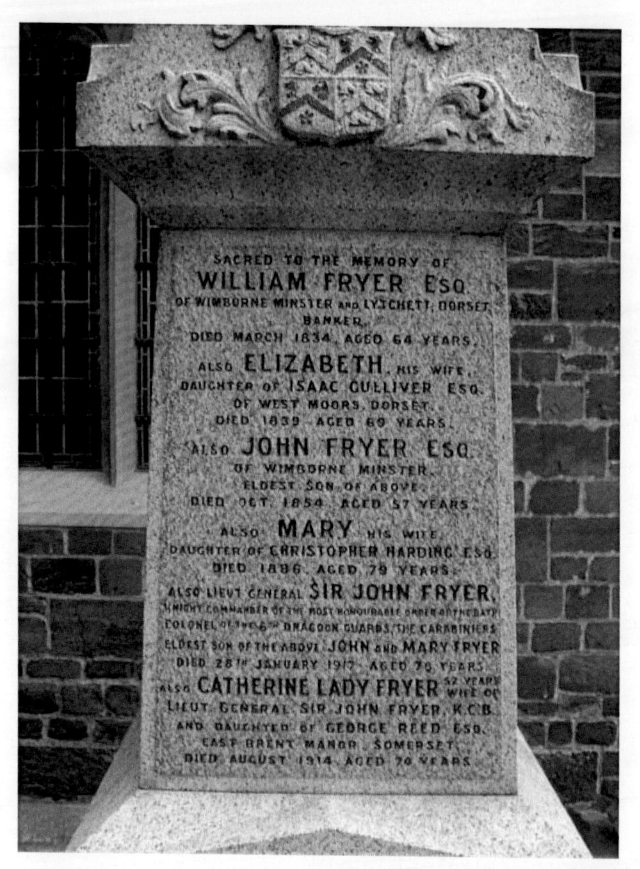

Tombstone of Gulliver's daughter Elizabeth Fryer

John Streeter (1750–1824)

John Streeter moved to the Christchurch area as a young man in 1773. There he met and married a local girl called Rose Button, a marriage that was to produce six children. By the age of twenty-nine, Streeter owned his own vessel, the *Phoenix*, which appears in revenue officer's records more than once. At the age of thirty-four he owned and ran a tobacco and snuff factory situated in Stanpit, Mudeford, next to the Ship in Distress, which at the time was run by a Hannah Sillers.

In 1786, aged thirty-seven, John Streeter was arrested and imprisoned for smuggling, only to escape from Winchester Gaol after bribing one of the guards. He fled to Guernsey, where he was exiled. In 1798 he took the advantage of the pardon being offered by the government of the time and returned. At the age of fifty-six, Streeter purchased a property in Stanpit called the Drakes. He died in 1824 at the age of seventy-four and was buried in the priory at Christchurch.

This is a potted history of John Streeter, a man that the custom officials at Cowes once described as a 'most notorious smuggler'. A more detailed look into the life and times of Streeter reveals a fascinating tale of crime and violence.

The first mention of Streeter in relation to smuggling was in the Letter Book from the custom house in London, but also featured in the Southampton custom house book from 1779. It mentions the vessel the *Phoenix*, since it had been seized on 1 July 1779 whilst lying in Christchurch Harbour. Streeter strongly denied that the ship was being used to run brandy, rum and gin, but in the end he accepted the charges and paid the fine of £55.

The next we hear of him is three years later in a report by William Arnold, in which it was recorded that smuggling in the area had increased greatly. His report mentions Streeter's vessel, the *Phoenix*, and its small cargo of brandy and tea that was landed at Hurst, Christchurch.

It appears that Streeter was illegally importing tobacco to support his tobacco and snuff factory at Mudeford. A report dated 17 June 1784 mentions a seizure of a 'hogshead of tobacco' by the riding officer from Christchurch. The tobacco was found in the cellar of a property owned by Streeter. The tobacco had been brought to him via a cart belonging to a known smuggler. When the documentation for the shipment was inspected, it was concluded that it had been tampered with: the name had been altered from Butlon (Streeter's brother-in-law) to Butlans. Furthermore, when the documents were fully checked the names did not tie up throughout.

At that point the revenue men suspected fraud. When weighing the tobacco, it was also found that it was 20lb over what the certificate claimed. Butlon's wife declared that the tobacco belonged to her husband, but luckily for him the prosecution failed due to a legal quibble and he went free, along with the tobacco which was released and restored to its owner.

The Ship in Distress, Stanpit, Mudeford

It was a common 'game' for smugglers to purchase a portion of tobacco legally and, in addition, purchase tobacco that had been seized from the public auctions. This then gave them invoices showing duty paid. If the stock of tobacco did not exceed the duty paid invoices then they were safe, but any excess tobacco had to be hidden away from prying eyes. Tobacco from different sources was very hard to identify so mixing in smuggled tobacco and legally purchased tobacco would have been easy.

July 1784 saw a significant milestone in the history of smuggling in Christchurch when a bloody clash between the revenue men and the smugglers occurred. 'The battle of Mudeford' was to go down in local history and ended with the death of custom man William Allen. The two vessels involved in the battle were the *Phoenix* and the *Civil Usage*. Both were owned by John Streeter.

In the aftermath of the clash, a list was drawn up by the revenue officers of suspected smugglers involved in the battle. John Streeter's name appeared prominently on this list. However, it was smuggler George Coombes, not Streeter, who was eventually hanged for the murder of William Allen; despite evidence suggesting that he had not fired the fatal shot.

Owing to his activities during the battle of Mudeford, and the fact that he was the owner of the two vessels used to smuggle contraband, John Streeter was sent to Winchester Gaol. Streeter was behind bars for two years before escaping with a fellow prisoner, Harry White, in 1786.

Streeter left the country to go into exile in Guernsey and Alderney. However, he used to make regular trips back to the mainland to see his wife and children, fathering two more children: William and Sukey. It appears that a man called John Early looked after Streeter's financial arrangements, tobacco and snuff factory and even his smuggling activities during his exile. On one of these return trips, Streeter was forced to evade capture by dressing up in a woman's cloak. Streeter eventually returned to the country a free man during the Napoleonic Wars, after taking advantage of the amnesty towards smugglers.

At the age of fifty-six Streeter retired, but not before suffering a parent's worst nightmare, between 1800 and 1805 he lost four of his six children: Edward in 1800 aged twenty-one; Rose in 1802 also aged twenty-one; James in 1803 aged eighteen; and Sukey in 1805, also aged eighteen. His remaining two children, John and William, survived him.

In 1806 at the age of fifty-six, John purchased the Drakes for £200 from John Le Mesurier. The property was adjacent to the Ship in Distress in Stanpit, and John probably spent many an hour at the inn. Could all the legends and old stories about the Inn be inspired by John himself and could the real 'ship in distress' in fact be John's vessel the *Phoenix*?

John Streeter died in 1824 at the age of seventy-four and was buried in the Priory Church at Christchurch.

Roger Ridout (1736–1811)

Roger Ridout was born in Farrington, in the parish of Iwerne Courtney in 1736. He was only child of William and Susanna Ridout, and grandson of Thomas Appowell of Fiddleford. When Ridout was ten years old, he and his cousin Elizabeth Clark inherited a leasehold dwelling house in Fiddleford along with some land at Sturminster Newton from their grandfather. But the last section of the will specified that each had to pay their mother £7 per annum from the proceeds. By the age of twenty Ridout was married to a woman named Mary, who gave him seven sons. Ridout's legitimate profession was as a miller, but he was best known for being a smuggler and stories abound of his exploits.

Ridout moved from Farrington to Fiddleford and then at some point moved to 'The Mills' on the Okeford Fitzpaine to Shillingstone Road, just north of Blandford Forum on the A357. Fiddleford Mill, one of Ridout's many hiding places can be found just off the A357.

Ridout and his gang seem to have been the haulage company of the time; they would collect the goods from the shoreline, normally Purbeck or the North Shore, and then with loaded wagons drive the cargo back through the narrow country lanes to Fiddleford Mill. From there they would move the goods to the surrounding farms. The whole community were involved and the tenants would leave the barton and stalls open, well-stocked with hay and straw, ready for Ridout and his fellow smugglers to hide the contraband where it could not be seen or found. The movement of these goods would have been like a highly organised military operation: armed men at the front and rear and the horses all tied together laden with contraband. Once in motion they would not stop for anything until they had reached their destination. Woe betide anyone who got in their way, the roads would have been narrow with very few places wide enough for two carriages to pass, definitely not two horses travelling at speed.

Tales of Ridout's exploits have travelled down through time for example: it is said that he owned a horse called Ridout's Ratted (or stumped) Tail and on one occasion as he arrived at Bridge Street in Sturminster Newton a mob of rival smugglers surrounded him and tried to pull him from his horse. Ridout is reputed to have leaned forward and whispered into the ear of the horse 'what would 'ee do fer thy king' on hearing this, the horse reared and kicked down the door of a nearby house so he could escape. There was extensive rivalry between the two smuggling gangs and Ridout was not always well-received in Sturminster Newton. On this occasion the Sturities (smugglers from Sturminster Newton) and the Okefordians (smugglers from Okeford Fitzpaine) clashed.

Another story recounts Ridout being lowered from the back window of his house in a bed sheet in order to avoid the revenue officers. However, he also tricked and evaded them in others ways. On returning one day from Fiddleford brewery with a bottle of balm he saw a revenue officer coming in his direction and knowing how inquisitive they were, Ridout shook the bottle of balm. As expected, the officer asked Ridout about the contents of the bottle. Deciding to play along, he asked the officer: 'Would 'ee like a smell?' He handed the bottle over and without thinking the revenue officer pulled the cork out of the bottle and instantly got a face full of balm. Ridout then pushed him into the ditch and went on about his business.

In 1787, Ridout also spent some time at His Majesty's pleasure in Dorchester Gaol. He was convicted of smuggling and fined £40. But seeing as his stay in Dorchester Gaol lasted for all of two weeks, he must have had the ability to pay the fine, or at least a wealthy benefactor willing to pay if for him. Ridout was lucky, because if you could not pay the money you were detained until the fine was paid or until the authorities decided to release you, which in some cases could take up to two years, depending on the severity of your crime. During his two week stay in Dorchester Gaol, Ridout's wife, Mary, walked the 40-mile round trip with a concealed bladder of brandy and a rubber tube. She would then pass the tube through the bars to her husband allowing him to have a drink, thus making his stay in prison that little bit more tolerable.

Later, in 1825, the Ridout's grandson, Joseph, who had followed on with the family business, was also caught smuggling and sent to Dorchester Gaol with a fine of £100, or twelve months behind bars if he could not pay.

The Okefordian gang of smugglers roamed around the area well into the nineteenth century. Apart from Joseph Ridout, there were two other smugglers from Okeford Fitzpaine who preceded him in Dorchester Gaol: Edward Marshalsay in 1813 and John Short in 1817.

The Poole custom records from 1774 show that the smugglers worked together on occasion. A report links the trio of Roger Ridout, William Beale and Isaac Gulliver, who were running 'great quantities of goods' on the North Shore. Then in 1778 Gulliver and Ridout are reported as working together again on the recovery of a cargo from Blandford. Were these two financially connected, with Gulliver bringing the goods in and Ridout distributing them? It is feasible that Ridout used Fiddleford Mills to hide the goods that Gulliver was bringing in.

Roger Ridout died at the age of seventy-five in 1811 and was buried at the local church, St Andrews, in Okeford Fitzpaine.

Okeford Fitzpaine

Okeford Fitzpaine

Okeford Fitzpaine

Ridout's Tombstone, St Andrews Okeford Fitzpaine

The Hawkhurst Gang (1735–1749)

The Hawkhurst Gang derived its name from their hometown of Hawkhurst in Kent. They first came to the public's attention in 1735 when they were known as the Holkhourst Gang and they soon developed into one of the most notorious of the age. In the early days the gang had the support of many of the local residents, but this changed after the raid on the Poole custom house in October 1747. Their exploits and influence took them from the Kent coast all the way down to the Dorset coast, spreading terror throughout the area as they went. However, their plundering was curtailed when their leaders were executed: Arthur Gray in 1748 and Thomas Kingsmill in 1749. This was a result of one of the most daring and vicious attacks on an informer and revenue officer ever seen.

The gang's main base was the Oak and Ivy Inn on the Sandhurst Road in Hawkhurst, but another local haunt was the Mermaid Inn in Rye, where they would sit with a loaded and cocked pistol on the table. The gang were always rowdy, and to maintain their fearsome and intimidating reputation, they would often fire their pistols into the ceiling of yet another inn, the Red Lion.

They were ruthless, as evidenced by their treatment of an informer who passed information over to the revenue men. The informant was taken to an island in a pool, where he was pegged out using straps leaving his head on the water's edge. When he was found the next day he was close to death, but survived, only to flee the area the next day. Another incident occurred in 1748 when a labourer was accused of stealing tea from the gang. He was kidnapped, and then was whipped and kicked in the groin until he died. His body was then thrown into a pond at Parkin Park.

Just the name Hawkhurst Gang struck fear and terror into the hearts of any who heard it. Their crimes and schemes were worse than any others of the time. Even the magistrates and the revenue officers would keep silent rather than run the risk of befalling one of the horrific ends meted out on the gang's victims.

The incident that saw the end of the gang, and resulted in their leaders being executed along with other members of the gang, took place in Poole, Dorset, in 1747. It all started on 22 September 1747 with the seizure of a cargo of 2 tons of tea, thirty-nine casks of brandy and a bag of coffee beans. These were seized from the smuggling vessel the *Three Brothers* by the revenue cutter *Swift.*

The *Three Brothers* was loaded with contraband and en route from Guernsey to a landing near Christchurch when the revenue cutter came across them. A chase ensued, which lasted six or seven hours and in the end the smugglers decided they had no chance of escape and surrendered. The cargo was seized, along with the vessel, which was taken to Poole, where the cargo was lodged at the custom house. The crew of seven aboard the *Three Brothers* included Jack Diamond, a former shepherd turned smuggler. He managed to escape capture and made his way back to the Hawkhurst Gang to let them know what had happened.

Also aboard the *Three Brothers* was Richard Perrin, who was the Hawkhurst Gang's buyer. He would normally have travelled to France to purchase the contraband. On this occasion however, it appears that the gang had a large stash of tea in Guernsey, which they had planned to sell on the South Coast. Unfortunately for Perrin word had got out about his plans and the revenue cutter *Swift* was out looking for them – and it found them.

The free members of the gang convened a council of war in Charlton Forest, at a spot called the Centre Tree on the Duke of Richmond's estate. A pledge was sworn to recover the goods, with Edmund Richards recording the names of all those present.

In total thirty men, including the gang's leader Thomas Kingsmill, members Jack Diamond and Richard Perrin, and an escaped prisoner called William Fairall, along with seven other members of the Hawkurst Gang, set off on 5 October 1747. After meeting at Rowlands Castle on the border of Hampshire and Sussex, they rode for about twenty-four hours to reach Lyndhurst where they stopped and rested, before setting out for their final destination of Poole.

On reaching the outskirts of Poole they sent in two men, Thomas Willis and Thomas Stringer, to scout the custom house.

Willis returned to inform the others of a sloop lying at the quay, with her guns trained on the custom's house door, which would have cut them to pieces had they attempted to attack. But before any decisions could be made, Stringer returned to inform the others that the tide had dropped and the threat from the sloop had gone.

With that, the raiding party mounted and moved into Poole. They rode down a little lane on the left side of the town, and came to the beach. Here they dismounted and left the horses. Perrin and a man named Thomas Lilliwhite were left to take charge of the horses – Perrin due to his rheumatism and Lilliwhite as it appears that this was his first outing with the gang.

Using hatchets and iron bars the gang smashed their way into the custom house and removed what had been taken from them, but no more. Making off with thirty-eight hundred weight of tea, they told the watchmen that 'they came for their own, and would have it, but would do no other.' The warehouse watchman then left to inform Mr Milner (the collector for Poole) of the events of the evening.

By morning the gang had reached Fordingbridge, where they stopped and had breakfast, and fed and watered their horses. The revenue officers were so enraged by the audacity of the attack that a large reward of £200 was offered (this was later raised to £500) for anybody who could provide any information towards the capture of any of the culprits. However, it appears that the Hawkhurst Gang's reputation preceded them and nobody came forward. If anybody had been brave enough to come forward, then how long would they have survived to enjoy their reward?

Sympathy for the smugglers' cause was high and by the time the gang were ready to resume their journey home a large cheering crowd had gathered. Jack Diamond recognised a member of the crowd as one Daniel Chater, a fifty-seven-year-old shoemaker. Diamond knew Chater from his days of harvesting, and with that he tossed the cobbler a bag of tea, an act that he would later regret.

Word of this act soon reached the ears of the revenue officers and Diamond was arrested and placed in Chichester Gaol. Chater was then ordered to testify against him before a judge. On 14 Febuary 1748, Chater left Fordingbridge to meet Major William Battine, a Sussex magistrate who was to take testimony from him regarding the events surrounding the Poole custom house break-in.

Chater was to be escorted by William Galley, a tidewaiter (a type of customs officer) from Southampton, to the magistrate in Sussex, but on the way they stopped at the White Hart at Rowland's Castle, a favourite drinking hole of the smugglers, an unfortunate coincidence for the two travellers.

The landlady, Elizabeth Payne, suspecting something was wrong, sent her son to fetch several of the smugglers. After plying them with several drinks of 'Hot', which was a mixture of gin and beer (a favourite drink of the smugglers), they extracted from Chater the exact purpose of their journey. Following a few more drinks the two travelling companions became rather drunk. The smugglers then took them to a room where they lay down and slept off the effects of the drink.

Whilst they slept the smugglers discussed what to do with them; regardless of anything their fate was not to be a good one. In the end they took both of them prisoner, intending only to hold them until after the trial of Jack Diamond, before subjecting them to the usual treatment afforded to informers. The two men were now in the hands of some ruthless and sadistic men – as they would soon find out.

The two men were woken in a most sadistic way with the aid of a pair of spurs to the forehead and a flurry of lashes from a horsewhip. Over the next few hours they were tortured and whipped mercilessly as they moved into the countryside. The two men were then put onto the back of a single horse. They were tied on and more than once they were turned upside down so that their heads were dragged along the ground beneath the horse's belly. Eventually they were placed onto individual horses, but Galley was so weak he had to be draped over the saddle.

The sorry parade continued until Galley fell from his horse and his captors, thinking he had died from a broken neck, decided to bury him. A grave was dug near Rake and he was placed in it, but it appears that he was not quite dead. When his body was eventually found there were signs that he had been buried alive: his hands were found to be covering his face as if to keep the dirt from his eyes and mouth.

Chater's fate was not much better. He was chained to a post in an outhouse belonging to Richard Mills, whose sons Richard and John actually took part in the raid on the custom house. He was left for the next forty-eight hours, whilst a decision was made on what was to be done with him. He was put through even more physical and verbal abuse and fed just enough to keep him alive. A decision was finally made to kill the poor man.

Chater's final resting place was a dry well at Ladyholt Park. His eyes were gouged out before he was hanged by the neck over the well using a cord supplied by Benjamin Tapner. After about fifteen minutes they threw him 30ft, head first, to the bottom of the well. However, thinking they could still hear him moaning and groaning the smugglers proceeded to throw down large rocks and a gatepost until the sounds stopped. When Chater's body was recovered, months later, it was discovered that one of his legs had been severed by rocks. The last thing that could incriminate the smugglers was the two horses. Galley's horse was slaughtered to hide the evidence, but luckily the horse that carried Chater escaped and returned to its owner at a later date.

As the news got around about the murders and the ruthlessness of the smuggler's actions, those who looked on the Hawkhurst Gang as benefactors soon started to turn against them. Gradually, one by one, the gang were captured, including their leader Thomas Kingsmill.

The first two to be arrested were William Steel and John Race, but both turned King's Evidence, earning a pardon and immunity. They became the principal prosecution witnesses, recounting the full story of the two murders.

Six months later an anonymous letter, which indicated where the bodies could be found, was delivered to the authorities. The bodies of the two men were uncovered and every effort was made to bring the culprits to justice. Over the next two years, thirty-five Kent and Sussex smugglers were hanged for offences, which also included the raid on Poole custom house and the murders of Galley and Chater; a further ten died in jail whilst awaiting execution.

The trials started in 1748 with William Carter, Jackson, Benjamin Tapner, John Cobby, John Hammond, Richard Mills senior and Richard Mills junior. All seven pleaded not guilty, but at the trial in Chichester they were found guilty and were subsequently executed. Out of the seven on trial, five were later gibbeted – hanged naked in chains outside their village as a warning to others as to what would happen if they followed the same life of evil.

In March 1749, Henry Sheerman (Little Harry) was tried at the East Grinstead Assizes and executed at Rake, close to where Galley was buried. His body was also gibbeted outside his village.

The leaders of the gang Thomas Kingsmill, William Fairall and Richard Perrin were tried at the Old Bailey in April 1749. They were all found guilty and executed. Their bodies too were gibbeted. Smugglers tended to fear gibbeting more than anything, knowing that they would be left to rot for all to see.

Jack Diamond, who started the whole debacle by passing that bag of tea to his friend, turned King's Evidence, saving himself from the gallows and earning his freedom.

Poole Customs House, Poole Quay

Slippery Rogers

Not much is known about Slipper Rogers beyond him being described as 'a celebrated adventurer in contraband articles'. His nickname, Slippery Rogers, came from his eel-like faculty of escaping the grasp of his maritime pursuer.

Rogers operated along the coast with a remarkable vessel of perfect symmetry and form. The ship was 120ft long, from the tip of her bowsprit and the end of her outrigger, with a cuddy fore and aft for sleeping berths. There was a large open space amidships for stowage of 2–3,000 ankers of spirits. She would travel at great speed powered by the thousands of square feet of canvas. Forty daring mariners would frequently row/sail the vessel across the channel on smuggling runs. They would set sail whatever the weather and face whatever nature had to throw at them.

One fateful evening, when the weather was closing in, and all sensible seamen were tucked up at home, Rogers and his crew left the Port of Le Havre with a full cargo of contraband. As they made their way towards the South Coast, the wind got up and the sea became very rough. The crew made for the shore but soon realised a landing was impossible. The waves pushed the vessel onto the beach in so doing the ship was bilged and shattered and ultimately lost. The cargo and some of the crew were swallowed by the sea and lost for good. They may well have hit the Beerpan Rocks just off Hengistbury Head.

Local tradition says that Slippery Rogers was the grandson of Henry Rogers, Mayor of Christchurch, who was either the author or preserver of the puzzling epitaph in the town churchyard:

We are not slain but raysed
Raysed not to life, but to be buried twice by men of strife.
What rest could living have, when dead had none?
Agree amongst you now, we ten are one.

John Rattenbury (1778–1844)

John Rattenbury was not truly a Dorset smuggler but his activities around Dorset warrant a mention. Originally from Beer in Devon, he was born in 1778 and baptised on 18 October 1778 being named after his father, John, a shoemaker, or as they were known in those days, a cordwainer. However, he never knew his father as before he was born John Rattenbury senior boarded a man-o'-war leaving his expectant wife behind, he was never heard of again and nobody knows what became of him.

At the age of nine, Rattenbury went off to sea as an apprentice on his uncle's boat. He was the youngest on board and as such was treated badly. One day at Lyme he was thrashed so badly by his uncle over an incident of negligence that he left the boat at Brixham. Finding a boat bound for Beer (his home port) he asked the captain for passage home. The captain agreed but upon his return, Rattenbury found that there was no work. He moved on and made his way to Bridport, where he found a coastal vessel working the route from Bridport to Dartmouth.

Rattenbury learned his mercantile trade as a seaman, travelling around the European ports and the Americas. On his travels he would have visited Guernsey and Alderney, places that would later play a vital role in Rattenbury's life. The Channel Islands, despite being closer to the French coast than the British, were loyal to the British sovereign. As a reward the islands were allowed to keep their own laws and customs; importantly for smugglers, the Channel Island ports were not subject to British custom law. Thus, foreign goods purchased here were not subject to duty or British taxes; it was only when the goods were landed on British soil that the duty/tax was payable.

At the age of nineteen, Rattenbury was once again looking for work and took employment on the vessel *Friends*, the master of which was Thomas Jarvis. *Friends* sailed on 17 March 1798 bound for Tenby, but during the voyage the vessel was taken by a French privateer. However, the British crew tricked the French by telling them that Alderney was in fact the English coast, and they even convinced them into lowering a boat ready to go ashore. Seeing his chance, Rattenbury fell overboard, swam ashore, and raised the alarm. The revenue cutter *Nancy* was in Swanage Bay and *Friends* was recaptured and taken into Cowes, the French privateers were captured and imprisoned.

On 17 April 1800, at the age of twenty-one, Rattenbury married eighteen-year-old Anne Partridge in Lyme. Living in Lyme and again unable to find work, Rattenbury joined a privateer, the *Alert*. The *Alert* weighed 117 tons and sailed from Weymouth with a crew of forty-five. Around 28 April 1800 she was awarded her letter of Marque. She was built by Nicholas Bools and William Good of Bridport and was captained by Thomas Diamond. The owners were hoping to come across a Spanish vessel. On returning to the Port of Weymouth in 1801, Captain Thomas Diamond was replaced by Captain Thomas Chiles.

Back in Lyme, the Rattenburys settled down and had their first child on 27 December 1801. The next few years were spent avoiding the press gang and staying out of trouble.

Rattenbury's next vessel was the *Unity*, an old smuggling vessel with a crew of thirty seized along with its cargo in 1803, and taken to Falmouth before being sold to Joseph Horsford of Weymouth. She was correctly registered on 11 December 1804 and awarded a letter of Marque.

During this voyage on the *Unity*, Anna Rattenbury gave birth to their second child Frances Nicholas. She was baptised in Lyme on 3 June 1805 and named after Anna's mother.

In August 1805, at the age of twenty-six, John Rattenbury's smuggling career really began. Before this, Rattenbury made his living through honest means: piloting, privateering and fishing – but these were boring. So, to inject a little interest and fun into his life, Rattenbury took part in some small-time smuggling, which was a lot more profitable than earning an honest living. However, this would bring him into conflict with the local revenue officers.

After returning from his privateering voyage aboard the *Unity*, Rattenbury's next two trips were not over to the Channel Islands but to Christchurch to fetch contraband. It looks like he made two trips: the first was successful but on the second they came up against the tender *Roebuck* and were captured. However, Rattenbury's luck was with him once more. During the confusion, as the revenue men attempted to board the *Roebuck* a man named Slaughter accidently blew his arm off whilst firing at Rattenbury. Seeing his opportunity, Rattenbury hid on deck until he could slip overboard and swim ashore. But Rattenbury was not one to leave his comrades behind; he returned and rescued his colleagues before making off with three kegs of brandy. They landed at Weymouth and then made their way home, happy with their victory in outwitting the revenue officers.

By this time, Rattenbury was a full-time smuggler with many interests. Generally, he was either directly involved with smuggling or was involved as a financier, backing and organising the trips. Rattenbury's main routes would have been between Cherbourg or the Channel Islands and the Dorset or Devon coast, with a varied cargo of kegs of spirits, lace and silks. Many would be in watertight kegs or boxes all ready to be sunk (you could purchase fully prepared kegs ready for sinking), and then collected at a later date when the revenue officers were not around.

Rattenbury also dealt in boats, but as always there was an alternative motive, he dealt in boats so as they would not be recognised and keep the revenue men on their toes. Rattenbury was a very lucky man, escaping arrest as many times as he was captured. On one occasion, he narrowly escaped prison for trying to repatriate French prisoners of war.

But Rattenbury was not always smuggling. You may say he was an early coastguard, putting to sea in dangerous conditions and piloting ships in distress into port; he saved the *Linskill*, a transport vessel. He would later earn respect and protection from the law for his skill and bravery.

In 1809, deciding to settle down again, Rattenbury took a career change and became a publican, but this didn't last for long, he was back to his old ways within a couple of years. In 1813, he gave up the pub, despite having a wife and four children to support. He worked where he could: piloting vessels in and out of port and then for a two-month period, along with his eldest son, worked a fishing boat out of Bridport for a wage of 27*s* a week for the pair of them. John's next vessel was the *Volante*, bought for a sum of £200. Using this vessel, Rattenbury started smuggling again: collecting cargo from Cherbourg and crossing the channel back to the Dorset coast. After losing the *Volante* in about 1816, Rattenbury managed to salvage and purchase another sloop called the *Elizabeth & Kitty*. He let this vessel out for fishing and then in 1817, as a passenger on his own sloop, sailed to Cherbourg, where he hired a French vessel to return to England with a cargo. Having arrived safely in England, he sent the French vessel back home.

In 1817, Rattenbury divided his sloop into shares and with partners made seven more voyages – all but one was successful. On returning from their second voyage they sank the cargo, but a strong storm and bad weather caused the kegs to break free and the revenue officers were able to collect most of them. The rest of the voyages went well and following the seventh, once all the goods had been disposed of, Rattenbury decided to lay the boat up.

By 1818, Rattenbury had fathered five children, William, aged sixteen, Frances Nichols, aged twelve, John Partridge, aged eight, Ann, aged five and finally Abraham Henry, aged one. John was also by now, at the age of thirty-nine, laid up with a severe case of gout.

Recovering the *Elizabeth & Kitty* in 1819, Rattenbury and his partners went out smuggling again, but on this occasion they came across a boat from the Greyhound commanded by Lt Anderson, the chase was on, tubs were thrown overboard and John Gover commander of Greyhound's other boat was tasked in collecting the tubs. John Gover found none of the tubs, but a local fisherman from Portland, Robert

White, picked them up and handed them over to John Gover and then claimed salvage; was he in league with John Rattenbury? Nobody will ever know for sure.

Rattenbury's next smuggling trip at the beginning of 1820 was not so successful: in fact, it ended up with the loss of the vessel and a cargo of thirty-four casks. To make matters worse, his son, William, and the rest of the crew were captured and convicted of smuggling and then sent to Dorchester Gaol. However, looking at the gaol register it appears that William was released after two months. The prison records describe William thus: 'very dark brown hair, of dark complexion, dark hazel eyes and two pockmarks between the eyebrows and a slight cut over his left eye'. This would not be William's only visit to Dorchester Gaol: in 1823 he was imprisoned and subsequently impressed into the navy in 1832, along with his father, he was convicted and fined £100 or faced fourteen months in prison.

In 1820, John Rattenbury started operating out of Weymouth and working the *Elizabeth & Kitty* near Abbotsbury. But one stormy night during his time at Weymouth, a Lyme Packet was driven into port. That Saturday night the captain got seriously drunk, and as a result the passengers left him behind. Rattenbury and his partners took advantage of this free vessel and travelled to Cherbourg, collected a cargo and returned back to Salcombe Hill (not far from Sidmouth). There they hove the boat intending to land the cargo, but with the weather being so bad getting their contraband ashore was near impossible. Unable to make it back to the ship, Rattenbury decided to swim back to the shore and from there made it to Exmouth. The cargo of 120 kegs was eventually sunk and the captain, now the worse for wear, came back on board and threw the remaining kegs that had not been sunk, overboard. They were retrieved by the cutter that had brought the captain back to his ship. The revenue cutter *Scrouge* then retrieved the 120 sunken kegs and Rattenbury was rewarded for his information and assistance in capturing the vessel and cargo. Rattenbury's partners were taken to Exmouth and appeared before the magistrate but claimed only to be passengers and as such were set free. Two of his men pleaded their innocence and swore that the cargo was not theirs, but rather belonged to John Rattenbury.

Rattennbury carried on his smuggling activities throughout 1820, but the records show that he may have lost one or two cargoes to the commander of the *Scrouge*, Lt McCrea. The lieutenant wrote about Rattenbury's activities in November 1820 and the week before the capture of the Lyme Packet, he captured a cargo of eighty tubs off Otter Head. Then in November he discovered two more sunken cargoes: one consisting of eighty-eight tubs and the second of twenty-six tubs. Lieutenant McCrea, thinking that the smugglers might try and collect the sunken cargo decided to lay in wait to see if they would return. Sure enough they did; two vessels returned, one of which turned out to be the *Hannah*, a vessel belonging to John Rattenbury. He lost a vessel and to add to insult to injury he was shot at as well.

On 1 January 1821, without fully understanding the danger of being prosecuted for smuggling, Rattenbury, at the age of forty-eight, set sail for Cherbourg. There he collected a cargo and sailed back to English soil. However, on this occasion Rattenbury was tricked by a Richard Morgan and served with a writ whilst on board the *Scrouge*. He was charged with smuggling and bail was set at £4,500. A figure far beyond anything Rattenbury could afford. Not realising how precarious a situation he was facing into, Rattenbury had brought his two young sons with him on the *Scrouge*: John, aged eleven and Abraham, aged four. The two boys were returned home and then the boat set sail for Exmouth, from where Rattenbury was taken to Exeter. He was tried, found guilty and sentenced to serve time on the St Thomas ward in Exeter Gaol. But Rattenbury's luck continued and in August 1821 he was released under the Act of Grace of King George IV after serving only two months of his sentence. However, there is some confusion regarding his release date. There was an incident in Devon County Gaol which would have put him there in around 1824. Sadly, it appears that the records for this period have not survived and so it cannot be verified how long he was in prison.

Rattenbury's family by now was growing; it included: William, aged twenty-six; Francis, aged twenty-two; John, aged eighteen; Ann, aged fourteen; Abraham, aged eleven; Mary Ann, aged eight; and Elizabeth, aged five. His wife was also pregnant with Hannah.

At the age fifty-one Rattenbury changed sides and obtained a position as a crewman on-board the *Tartar*, a revenue cutter. He was a great asset to the revenue men as the former smuggler knew the coastline like the back of his hand. However, he only stayed on board for two months due to illness. After falling seriously ill, Rattenbury was taken to Weymouth and placed in the sick quarter until 6 January 1830.

But that wasn't the end for Rattenbury. He was again caught for smuggling on 18th November 1832 along with his son, William, and a number of other smugglers. He was fined £100 but because he was unable to pay the fine, he ended up in Dorchester Gaol for fourteen months. Looking at the records for both father and son, William's sentence was the same as his fathers, but in his case he was taken to the flagship in Portsmouth and impressed into the navy. However, luck was on William's side (maybe he had inherited his father's luck); he was found to be unfit for naval service and returned to Dorchester Gaol within a week. Over the next year they both petitioned for their release and in both cases they were refused on the grounds of their notoriety in the smuggling fraternity. Whilst in gaol, Rattenbury was employed as watchman by night and looked after the boys by day, with great success. This endeared him to the chaplain and governor, which, in turn, eased the hardships he had to endure whilst serving time in Dorchester Gaol.

Rattenbury was released from Dorchester Gaol on 1 February 1834. In March of the same year he was out smuggling again. As he had done on many occasions, he took a trip to Cherbourg to collect a cargo of spirits. Half of the cargo was sunk, and it appears a portion was lost, while the barrels that did come ashore were stashed for three days until Rattenbury could organise for them to be moved. His final voyage to Cherbourg was in October of the same year, but the cargo was lost to the revenue men. By 1835, the roles played by son and father had changed – Rattenbury was assisting his son, William, in landing and running contraband ashore and for a final time, Rattenbury was caught in the act, however his perennial luck prevailed and he again escaped a prison sentence.

Rattenbury's final appearance in court came in March 1836, when he acted as a witness for his son, William, who was being tried for an assault on a revenue officer in 1835.

In 1836 Rattenbury hung up his smuggling boots for the last time.

Rattenbury was a devoted family man and sadly lost two of his children long before their time: Hannah, aged six, in 1834; and Elizabeth, aged thirteen, in 1835. In 1844, at the age of sixty-five, John Rattenbury died. He was buried on 28 April.

During his lifetime, Rattenbury did many things, but one of his final actions was to write down all his exploits. The resulting transcript became his memoirs, which were published in 1837. Due to the fact that many of the people mentioned in the book were still alive and smuggling, their identities were changed so that they could be protected.

He survived many encounters with the revenue officers and had many adventures both legal and illegal; in my opinion, John Rattenbury was a remarkable person who must be admired for his ingenuity and quick thinking.

Sam Hookey (1725–1796)

Sam Hookey, or as he was known, the Wicked Man of Wick, was born near Wick Farm in 1725. Wick was a tiny village on the banks of the River Stour consisting of a few cottages built around a triangular village green. However, no pub or church could be found in this village. Hookey's father was a fisherman and, like so many in those days, supplemented his income by smuggling. Hookey was one of ten brothers and sisters; and his mother was a beautiful Spanish girl brought from Guernsey to England under duress by his father.

Hookey was fearless and impulsive and always had bright ideas from an early age. An example of his curious nature comes from a tale relating to when he was just a boy. Hookey would investigate the prehistoric mounds at Hengsitbury Head. These mounds were met with superstition and care, but not by Hookey. On one occasion his friends deserted him and left alone he somehow became trapped by a large rock across his legs. It was only after many hours lying pinned to the ground that he was discovered by a passer-by who heard his cries for help. Though freed, Hookey was left with a severely deformed leg.

His first job was as a ferrier. He served his apprenticeship but then set up his own smithy – the location of which is thought to be down the end of Pound Lane in Christchurch. But like father like son, Hookey apparently also supplemented his income with smuggling. He gathered a reputation as a ruthless and fearless smuggler, crossing swords on many occasions with the revenue officers and taking part in many a run.

One of the most infamous of Hookey's exploits, so the story goes, occurred one night in 1764 at Whitsuntide. Whilst on a smuggling run, Hookey decided to split his forces into two parts. The smaller of the two forces was sent to the mouth of the River Bourne, where they ran ashore a few tubs of brandy. The riding officer and supervisor for the area got wind of this and went to intercept and seize the cargo. The smugglers put up a fight, but in the end they were overrun. However, the riding officers decided to open the tubs they'd seized, only to find that they were full of seawater.

Whilst this was going on, Hookey was landing the real cargo. Hookey and his main force of men, consisting of three luggers in full sail and forty oarsmen made their way through Christchurch Harbour and up the River Stour to where Wick Ferry is situated today. The area at the time was marshland, but today it has all been developed and built on. With the help of many of the locals they unloaded about 12,033 tubs of foreign spirits, approximately 2 tons of tea and two bales of silk.

In the days when this run took place nearly everybody in the area would have been involved and the contraband would either have been moved straight inland to awaiting customers or secreted in the many hiding places in the area, like St Andrews Church in Kinson. In fact, this may have even been the biggest run to have taken place at the time off the English coast.

Hookey was so prevalent in the smuggling scene in Dorset, that if there were any smuggling or goods being run then he was either the one doing the smuggling, or was involved in some other capacity. Hookey also owned three vessels which he kept in Christchurch Harbour. And being a smithy he could have made all the tools of his trade i.e. the long pole grappling irons used to retrieve sunken tubs.

One of Hookey's identifying features was his eye patch which covered an eye lost in a battle with the authorities. He wore a leather eye patch which he apparently never removed in forty years from the day he lost his eye.

Hookey became a very wealthy man and also a pillar of the community. During his life he served as mayor twice: in 1727 and 1743. Alas, he was also quite free with his earnings and spent money as quickly as he earned it – living life to the full. He was respected by his peers and throughout his smuggling career he was noted as being a good organiser and also a good leader of men – always getting the best from his crew.

Hookey lead a full and colourful life and he died doing what he liked best: smuggling. At the ripe old age of seventy-one he made his last run. On the night of 29 August 1796, whilst running tea, lace and gold across the River Stour just up from Wick Ferry, he was disturbed by Preventative Men. In an attempt to escape, Hookey wandered off line and fell into a deep hole. He was weighted down with the gold belts around his waist and he sank to the riverbed and drowned. His body was never found, nor was the gold he was carrying.

Today, when the weather conditions match those of the night when Hookey died, it is said that a ghostly figure can be seen beating the water on the spot where he drowned. It is known as Hookey's Hole.

A search for the treasure of Sam Hookey took place in 1954. Three local divers searched the riverbed for two hours before a crowd of 200 onlookers – even the BBC was present. They found several deep holes and in one of them they found a gold coin dated 1710, but no Hookey.

Strange as it might sound the whole story of Sam Hookey is an interesting one but one that was fabricated by Mr Warner of Wick Holiday Camp. In 1954 he decided to build a club house on the holiday camp called 'Hookey's Club' and so made up a smuggling story around the club which was printed within a pamphlet. Although Sam Hookey was a real person living in Wick and was once the Mayor of Christchurch his smuggling exploits were not based on real facts.

Robert Trotman (Died 1765)

The death of Robert Trotman occurred on 24th March 1765, and involved a gang of twenty smugglers who were running a cargo of tea. As they were loading the cargo onto their horses they were discovered by Lt Down and fourteen hands from the cutter *Folkestone*, which at the time was lying off Brownsea Island.

First on the scene was an unfortunate midshipman who was mercilessly beaten with horsewhips by the smugglers. He was then dragged down to the sea and left to drown, but luckily he managed to drag himself out of the water before hiding in one of the chines. Lieutenant Down met with a similar fate to the midshipman, but he was also wounded by a pistol shot. The lieutenant then gave the order to cut the bags of tea from the horses, but the smugglers were resolute and horsewhipped any who came close; another person was shot and wounded in the leg.

Trotman's gravestone in St Andrews Church Kinson

The smugglers then tried to rescue the tea and during the ensuing battle the leader of the smugglers, Robert Trotman, was killed. As it was dark Lt Downs was not sure who had fired the fatal shot.

Strangely, the coroner was sent for from Ringwood by the smugglers and not by Lt Downs. The next afternoon the inquest was held and as implausible as it might sound the jury were allegedly smugglers, and they returned a verdict of 'Wilful Murder by person or persons unknown'.

Robert Trotman is buried in St Andrews Church in Kinson and on the headstone has been carved the following epitaph:

> To the Memory of Robert Trotman
> Late of Rond in the county of Wilts who was barbarously murdered on
> Shore near Poole the 24th March 1765 the
> A little tea, one leaf I did not steal
> For Guiltless bloodshed I to God appeal
> Put tea in one scale, human blood in the other
> and think what 'tis to slay a harmless brother

Emmanuel Charles (1781–1851)

Emmanuel Charles was born on 17 January 1781 to Henry and Mary Charles. He was baptised in Osmington Church on 20 February 1781.

Charles became the leader of a gang of smugglers that used the Crown at Osmington Mills as their headquarters; at one time Charles was also the landlord. He was quite a character, fearless when it came to facing down the revenue men and woe betide anybody that got in his way. However, for Charles smuggling was a family business. He worked alongside his brother, cousins, other relatives and ultimately his sons.

Charles used to smuggle brandy into the country, but it was so bad that not even the locals would drink it. He had to have it redistilled in the brew house to the rear of the pub before it could be consumed or sold.

In 1804 Charles married Elizabeth Hardy of Puncknowle. He met Elizabeth in 1800 and apparently she initially wanted nothing to do with him. In fact, it is said that she 'broomsticked' him with a broom. In the year following their marriage, Charles was press-ganged to serve in the Napoleonic Wars.

Their marriage yielded thirteen children and the first, Richard, was born in 1809. It was no surprise that he followed in his father's footsteps. In 1828, at the age of nineteen, whilst aboard the *Integrity* and under the direction of his father, Richard was caught smuggling, and subsequently appeared in front of the magistrate at Poole. His sentence was to be 'impressed into the navy'.

His father went to great lengths to have the decision overturned; petitioning the treasury on the grounds that Richard's health, he claimed, was of, 'consumptive habit of body and decaying constitution'. He was so determined that he even brought testimony from George Ellis senior and George Ellis junior, both surgeons from Weymouth. He backed up these affidavits with another from a George Willoughby of Weymouth, who attested to the good character of the Ellis men. Affidavits were also produced from William Voss, a blacksmith, which showed that Richard's apprenticeship indenture had been cancelled, 'in consequence of his ability to make use of anybody exertion'. Charles even offered to pay the sum of £100 to the commissioners of the treasury if they would discharge his son.

The petition was duly considered and the treasury then passed it onto the custom board at Poole and then onto the collector and Comptroller at Poole. They made the point that the vessel on which he had been caught was in no way a fishing vessel, rather it was a smuggling vessel, and had been for many years. Richard had been employed on the *Integrity* for at least three years, and 'no other vessel similarly employed has been so successful'. Richard also appears to have passed all the medical examinations at Poole and Portsmouth.

In a closing statement customs said that: The petition was refused.

> We cannot forbear expressing our gratification at the capture of the son of the petitioner who under his father we have little hesitation in stating lent his aid in the serious opposition which the coastguard have recently experienced in this neighbourhood and the father himself we are led to believe, is the organiser of the armed desperate gangs which infest this coast in aid of the smuggler.

The Crown Inn now known as the Smugglers Inn,
Osmington Mills, Weymouth

Charles did everything in his power to stop his son being impressed into the navy but in the end he failed. Richard served his time and afterwards returned to the family business of smuggling. However, in the end he paid the ultimate price for smuggling and was shot dead by Poole customs officers.

Charles and other members of his family also seem to have spent their time in Dorchester gaol, as evidenced by the prison records. In fact, it appears there were twenty-seven convicted smugglers in the family. Some served time, some were fined (they paid), while others were impressed into the navy. The fines imposed were around £100 and the punishment for failure to pay would have been between three and eighteen months behind bars.

Charles' final gift was Radipole House, built on the bank of the backwater at Radipole in Weymouth. But things must have changed for Charles because he died at the age of seventy whilst living with his son Israel, who described him as being in an 'impoverished state'.

The Crown Inn still stands today, although it is now known as the Smugglers Inn and sits amongst the surrounding cottages and houses.

Female Smugglers

Mother Sillers and the Ship in Distress

Hannah 'Mother' Sillers, or as she was also known, the Angel of the Marsh, was one of the main proponents of smuggling in the area.

It all began when Hannah married John Sillers, landlord of the Haven House, Mudeford, in Christchurch Priory. With the death of her husband in 1780 she took over the inn and became the landlady. Hannah came from an old family of innkeepers; her grandfather was the landlord of the Lamb at Holfleet near Winkton and so, taking over from her husband and running the Haven House would have been no problem to her.

Hannah played a pivotal role in the Battle of Mudeford in 1784. Later, she became the landlady of the Ship in Distress, which was positioned

Mother Siller's Channel, Stanpit Marsh, Christchurch Harbour

Mother Sillers Channel, Christchurch Harbour

on the edge of Stanpit Marsh (an area covering 65 acres on the eastern side of Christchurch Harbour), a move that would thrust her deeper into the world of smuggling. This was a remote and dangerous place, rarely visited by customs men. Smugglers could float their cargo from the harbour up the channel behind the inn, right up to Mother Sillers' back door. She could then pick and choose what she wanted from them, and the smugglers knew they had somewhere safe to rest. Today this channel, still named after her, is nothing like what it was. In those days it was navigable and safe for smugglers but two centuries of silt have turned it into a slow-running creek that disappears into the marsh reeds.

Hannah would signal to the smugglers by wearing a red cloak, indicating that it was safe to bring the cargo ashore. In her role as watcher Hannah became much loved and was dubbed 'the protecting angel of all smugglers'. From the inn, smugglers could carry on along the routes out of the county. Their next stop would have been the Fisherman's Haunt at Winkton and then on to the Lamb, Hannah's old family inn. At each inn they would have made a sale or have stashed cargo before moving on. From the Lamb, they would have travelled on to the Three Tuns at Bransgore and from there onto Thorney Hill and into Burley where they would call at the Queen's Head.

It also appears that Hannah fell in love with a smuggler whilst she was running the Ship in Distress. Billy Coombs was the captain of the *John and Susannah*, a smuggling vessel, and sometimes privateer, that weighed 100 tons, and which was armed with fourteen cannon. He left Hannah for a smuggling trip with the promise that upon his return he would give up smuggling and privateering, settle down with her and become the landlord of the Ship in Distress. To show his intent he left her with some private and personal papers.

Hannah being curious decided to take a look at these papers and found amongst them bills and promissory notes, and a love letter sent to Billy from a young lady in Hamble, Billy's home port. Like Hannah, she too had been promised marriage and a settled, sober life.

Upset over the love letter, she decided to inform the preventers of Billy's trip and when he would return. Billy sailed into the harbour unaware of what awaited him: the *Osprey*. A three-hour battle ensued, as broadsides rang from both sides. Billy's vessel, *John and Susannah*, was badly battered and dismasted. Then, without Billy's orders, someone decided to pull down their colours as a gesture of surrender, however, instead of surrendering, Billy carried on fighting. His actions were considered a serious breach in the rules of engagement and would seal his fate. When the battle was over and all the crew had been securely locked away, Billy, as captain, was tried and hanged, at Stoney Pointe, Lepe, just across Southampton Water from his home port of Hamble.

Lovey Warne

Our next lady of smuggling is Lovey Warne or, as she sometimes called, the Lady in Red. She earned this name by standing on Vereley Hill, near Burley, in a bright red cloak. Unlike Hannah Sillers, when the smugglers saw her standing there they knew that the revenue men were about and so they were careful to stay off the well-trodden paths used to move their illegal cargo inland. In the late eighteenth and early nineteenth century the New Forest was awash with smugglers and Lovey Warne was doing them all a good service by warning them of impending danger. But at night a lantern would be lit and hung on the hill, normally tended by others, so that Lovey could join her brothers on one of their many runs.

Lovey led an exciting life working alongside her brothers, smuggling in silks and fine materials. Not one to just follow, Lovey was known to go down to meet the ships as they landed. She would then go on board, take off her dress and wrap herself with silks and fine materials before covering them with her voluminous dresses. Lovey managed to avoid any contact with the authorities but then one day, an amorous revenue officer invited her out for a drink at Ye Olde Eight Bells in Church Street. Not wishing to arouse suspicion she accepted; after a few gins the revenue officer placed his hand on Lovey's knee, and in response she jumped up and jabbed the lecherous officer in the eye with her elbow. The landlady saw what had happened and came over to see what she could do. She tended to the officer whilst Lovey made good her escape. From that point on, Lovey decided not to go down to the ships anymore and ended her career as a smuggler.

Lovey never married and lived in a cottage with her brother, Peter, not far from Burley. The cottage then was called Beautiful Views and was situated at Knaves Ash, halfway between Crow and Burley, not far from the old smugglers' road that ran across the heath towards Vereley Hill. Today the cottage is known as Knaves Ash.

Her other brother, John, lived about ½ mile closer to Ringwood in a cottage that is known as Halfway Cottage today. As many people who lived in and around the New Forest had two occupations, John and Peter were not only smugglers but also maltsters. Their malthouse apparently still stands today at Knaves Ash and can be seen from the road.

Peter died in 1870 and in his will he left instructions that Lovey could live in the cottage until her death, after which the cottage was to go to William Burnetta, a timber merchant living in New Zealand.

Lovey carried on living in the cottage until her death in 1873 at the ripe old age of eighty-four. In her will she left the princely sum of £6 (clearly in her case smuggling did not pay well), which was to be divided between George Blandimore of the Crow, whom she left £2, her niece from Surrey who received £1, the remainder went to Henry Dear Holloway, son of the head keeper at Holmsley Lodge.

By the time of Lovey's death in 1873 smuggling had virtually been stamped out. There were widespread changes in the law and many acts against smuggling had been put in place. The Act of 1848, in particular, had a great effect. Many of the goods that had had duty applied to them were taken off the statutory book, and more and more power was given to the revenue men to aid them in searching out and catching the smugglers. Thus smuggling became a less profitable business and those who continued to flout the laws were in greater danger of being caught and punished.

Other Notable smugglers of Dorset

There are many other smugglers who deserve a mention: Bone Tucker, John Early and Abraham Pearson, in 1739 the parish clerk at the village of Steep, carpenter by day and smuggler by night.

John Sinick, leader of the Studland gang, who waged a vendetta against the local customs boatman, Thomas Hutchin.

Looking further to the west around Osmington Mills there was a notorious French smuggler called Pierre Latour, or French Pete as he was known. His headquarters were the Crown Inn which, as it so happened, was also the home to another notorious smuggler, Emmanuel Charles. Pierre and his vessel *L'Hirondelle* were sought by the revenue men and Pierre must have been quite prolific in his exploits because he had a price on his head.

Robert Gillingham was a smuggler from Bere Regis who, in 1778, along with his fellow smugglers, rescued a cargo of brandy and rum that had been seized. In the 1780s, Bere Regis was a dangerous place, full of notorious smugglers and as such it was very difficult for the revenue men to apprehend Gillingham. After two years of trying they still could not serve a writ on Robert, he would not accept it, 'declaring he will never be served'.

The Dorchester Gaol register lists whole families of smugglers: fathers, sons, daughters and even mothers. One such family were the Beales, who had connections to Roger Ridout and Isaac Gulliver. Then there are the Pearces from Portland; forty-year-old Susan and her fifteen-year-old daughter, Rebecca, served time in Dorchester Gaol on charges of smuggling. The prison records show that the majority of smugglers came from places like Portland, Weymouth and coastal villages which is hardly surprising given that many of the smugglers were also fishermen.

Martha Hurdle was caught in 1816 attempting to smuggle shawls, handkerchiefs, gloves and lace, all of which carried a heavy duty. When captured she was carrying:

1 silk shawl

4 silk half hankies

13 silk hankies

24 pairs of leather gloves

1 silk lace shawl

2 silk lace half shawl

The value of the goods was £13 11*s* but she also had 20 yards of lace which was valued at £5 5*s*. The report went on to say that she had to forfeit a sum of £58 8*s*, which was about three times the value of the goods seized, but that was not the end of it, she was also ordered to appear in front of a Justice of the Peace.

Famed novelist and poet, Thomas Hardy, had connections to smuggling through his grandfather, Thomas. In the 1800s, his grandfather lived in an isolated cottage at Higher Bockhampton in Puddletown. At any given time, he would have had about eighty tubs, each containing 4 gallons of spirits, hidden in a dark closet. The tubs were delivered in the dead of night, a whiplash across the windowpane letting Thomas know that the smugglers had arrived. Having dressed and gone downstairs he was met by a pile of kegs at the door. In the end his wife persuaded him to stop smuggling. By 1805 he had told the smugglers to stop dropping off the kegs, but it was harder to persuade the smugglers to stop. Even after many years, a very large woman known as Mother Rogers would stop by and ask if they wanted anything cheap; her size was due to the bullock's bladders slung around her hips filled with spirits.

Another name that comes to mind is Lewis Tregonwell. The 'Founder of Bournemouth' as he was known, was a famous and well-known character in the town. Whether or not he was involved in smuggling no one will ever know for sure as all the evidence is circumstantial; nothing ties him directly to the local trade. Tregonwell knew the area very well, having patrolled the Dorset coast as the commander of the Dorset Rangers from 1796–1802, when a French invasion was feared. This would have afforded him a great knowledge of where to land cargo and where to hide it. Also, having served in the army he would have known how the authorities would have thought and acted.

The main evidence which suggests Tregonwell's involvement in the smuggling trade was the chamber found when the house he had built for his butler, Symes, was demolished. The chamber was 10' x 8' x 6', and when it was uncovered it had been set about a foot or so underground. When opened the chamber collapsed, filling in, but in Tregonwell's defence it was not that large, very little could have been hidden in it. Indeed, it may just have been for storage, like a wine cellar or somewhere to store food like a modern cold room. Tregonwell also acted like he had nothing to hide; instead of keeping people away from the area, he encouraged people into it by letting out the properties he had built. Whether or not he was involved with the smugglers we may never know, but he did have the perfect cover and all the opportunities required to carry out the act.

Halfway Cottage, Knaves Ash

Vereley Hill, Burley
Lovey Warne would stand here in her red cloak

Lewis Tregonwell's Portman Lodge

Abraham Pike's residence, 10 Bridge Street, Christchurch

3
The Life of a Riding Officer at the turn of the nineteenth century

Abraham Pike

We have looked at the industry through the eyes of a smuggler, but what about the experiences of the preventative officers. We are very lucky to be able to glimpse into the life and times of a preventative officer in *The Supervisor of Customs and Coast Waiter*, the journal of Abraham Pike. Coast Waiter meant that he would have had to oversee the unloading and loading of cargo from the ships that docked at Christchurch Quay and the Haven at the mouth of Christchurch Harbour.

Normally the riding officer's journals, when completed and checked by the supervisors, would have been destroyed. However, the journals of Abraham Pike from 1803–1804 survived and came to light when a quantity of books and waste-paper were purchased from the Pikes' family home in Bridge Street in 1917. These journals are now kept in the Red House Museum in Christchurch.

Riding officers faced long days and long nights, without rest and in all weathers. There was no time off, even on Sundays, and the job was not without its degree of danger. Pike's journal does mention a few encounters with the smugglers, but the job could also be extremely boring; just riding around, often alone, up and down the Dorset coastline and roads looking for any signs of the smugglers.

A look through Pike's journal shows how big an area he was expected to survey. To do this effectively he met up with his fellow officers every few days, so that they could patrol and survey the area together. Pike's jurisdiction covered the coastal area from Parkeston to Mineway and also quite a way inland. There are also mentions of him going into the New Forest as far as Thornhill (Thorny Hill as it is known today) and in Pike's day this area would not have been inhabited. Other areas he travelled to on his daily grind included: Sandford, Small Ford, Barnfield, Vernhill, Parley, Crow, Hurn, the Avon Causeway, and

Burley. He would also have travelled along the coast around his hometown of Christchurch, and on towards Bournemouth, Alaman (Alum Chine) and Beacon North.

In Pike's time the area would have been totally different – Bournemouth did not exist and the land between Poole and Christchurch was just rough heath.

The journal entries detailed the route Pike would have taken, the reason for it and whether or not he saw any action. For example: '[travelled] coast to the East [or West]', 'on discoveries', but they mostly finished with 'no success' or 'nothing found'. In fact, there are just six success stories in the two years that his journal covers. When he did make a seizure, the goods would have been taken and secured in Poole Custom House, being the closest bonded warehouse to Christchurch, (his residence, No.10 Bridge Street, did have a cellar that was capable of storing goods, but it was only used while they were waiting to transport the contraband to Poole Custom house).

Overseeing the unloading and loading of the many vessels that frequented Christchurch Harbour an entry in 1803 explains that he, 'went to Haven on coast duty, sending of wheat from Chichester', and in the same month he also 'went to Quay on coast duty, shipping of beer and malt from Portsmouth'. These types of entry appear at least once or twice every month, indicating how busy this little harbour used to be. However, one of the downfalls of the harbour was its narrow entrance, commonly known as the Run. When the tide was running out it was very difficult to enter the harbour. There was also a moving sandbar at the entrance to the harbour, and it had a tendency to silt up as two rivers – the Stour and the Avon – meet in the harbour. These factors limited the size of vessel able to use the harbour.

Pike's records show that Christchurch relied heavily on deliveries by sea, with commodities such as coal arriving from Portsmouth or Southampton, wheat from Chichester, beer and malt from Portsmouth. Items such as tea and candles, and other commonly used products, came in from further afield. Then there were the more unusual items as an entry from March 1803 shows. Pike was called to the quay to oversee the landing of bricks and tiles from Lymington. At the same time, he also had to oversee the loading of produce and goods leaving Christchurch.

From the entries, it appears that Pike was not only a riding officer, but also a supervisor. Each month, he visited a group of preventative men to examine and sign their journals, comparing the details and ensuring that they corresponded. One such entry is shown below:

> Surveyed the west coast met with Mr Wise with whom surveyed the road to my residence and read his journal for the month of September, afterwards examined my officers and signed their books and reviewed their journals for the month of September.

Despite the difficulty of his job, Pike did have a number of successes over the years. The first came in April 1803. His diary entry is telling and shows how reluctant the officer was to leave his warm and comfortable home at 1 a.m. to undertake the 32-mile round trip, which meant that he would not return until 4 p.m. the following day:

> Called on Mr Thos Lambert Boatman informing me he saw a boat in at Boskom (Boscombe) and landing her goods. Set out with my officers and a party, in the heath near Boskom seized two wagons and one cart with 250 casks of foreign spirits and tobacco and one case of playing cards, returned to Christchurch and called on Thomas Jeans Esq. and found James Williams with whom set out. Thomas Lambert and one soldier on horseback to the beach at Boskom where Thomas Lambert seized the boat and … On coming up from the beach met Mr James Williams and informed him the boat was seized and that I was going to Poole. Sent Messrs Preston and Jones with two soldiers to Boskom to get the boat and with Mr Bacon, Newman and soldiers went to Poole with the goods. Met Mr Preston, Jones and Lambert and secured the above seizure in his majesties warehouse. Corresponded with the principal officers. Captain of the 'Seagull' and Mr Wise surveyed the coasts home. Nothing else occurred.

When the revenue officers received information of a landing there was a rush to intercept and seize the contraband as happened in October 1803. Pike, a Mr Wise and twenty Light Dragoons, rushed to Bournemouth, reaching the area to find (in the heath and surrounding area) sixty-three casks of foreign spirits and one cask of tobacco. As usual, these goods were then taken and placed in the Poole Custom House. Fortuitously, on their way back home, they also seized two casks of cordial, one cask of spirits and a parcel of tobacco.

Another entry from 12 August 1804 reads as follows:

> First informed by Messrs Wheatley and Roberts, Excise officers, the smugglers had gone to the west shore, set out with the above officers and a party to the shore, found they had worked and gone off and at West Moors in the county of Dorset, 324 casks of foreign spirits, 2 wagons, 3 carts, 10 horses and harnesses. Secured the spirits at Weakley's residence; the wagons, carts, horses and harnesses at the barracks in Christchurch.

Another entry shows that Pike actually stopped the landing of a cargo on 15 October 1803. He left his home at 8 p.m., setting out for Wallisdown, searching the area for any signs of smugglers or hidden goods. Having found nothing, but knowing that the goods were somewhere in the area, he travelled to the beach at Boskom where he found the smugglers busy and on the lookout. However, on this occasion he was able to stop the landing and running of goods.

Pike was not alone in his duties. If he was called away, like when he was training with the cavalry in Southampton, he could rely upon a number of other officers to fulfil his duties. This included: Mr Prichard, the riding officer and collector from Lymington; Mr Howe and Mr Burgess, the excise officer and collector from Ringwood; and Mr Weakley, the excise officer from Wimborne. Pike could also call upon the cavalry stationed at the barracks in Christchurch, and at times he was grateful for their assistance in the pursuit of the smugglers.

Along with the knowledge that he could call on his fellow officers as required, he would have also drawn comfort from the fact that there was a revenue cutter patrolling the coast; first the *Batt*, under the command of Mr Williams and later, in 1804, the *Seagull*, under the command of Mr Carter. The cutters and the men on land would coordinate their efforts in trying to capture the smugglers, although, not always successfully.

One such joint venture occurred in October 1803; the entry reads as follows:

> Corresponded with the commander of the Batt cutter, afterwards surveyed the west coast to Aluman (Alum Chine) nothing occurred.

However, sometimes they were successful. For example, on the 14th April 1804, Mr Pike surveyed the east coast and met up with the commander of the *Batt* who informed him that a seized cargo of 300–400 kegs was on the cutter, *Speedwell* and that Mr Pritchard from Lymington had also made a small seizure.

The reality is that being a riding officer was an extremely tiring occupation. They could be called upon at any hour, in all weathers and were given very little time off. They worked very hard every day, enduring long periods of idleness punctuated with flashes of excitement and danger. Officers were known to have been captured, tortured and even thrown from the cliffs along the coast. There are records of men being thrown from the cliffs at Lulworth to the beach below and from High Downs straight to the sea.

On 21 September 1790, Pike and Henry Dale were attacked 5 miles from Sopley Common. They were knocked from their horses and then badly beaten. The incident was uncovered when their horses were found at Christchurch.

But it was not only the criminals which posed a threat to the health of the preventative men. Prolonged exposure to bad weather was part and parcel of the role, but it also took its toll. In 1799 Richard Newman, a riding officer at Christchurch, passed away. His demise was blamed on his continued exposure to bad weather over a number of winters.

Warren Lisle

An earlier revenue officer worthy of mention was Warren Lisle. Born in 1699, he was the son of George Lisle, the collector of customs at Lyme Regis. Lisle has been described as the scourge of the Dorset smugglers, and was, in fact, a very conscientious, thorough and hardworking officer, with a career that led him to be very wealthy and influential.

His career started in 1718, at the age of just seventeen, when he became the patent searcher in the Port of Poole. Within the year he had fathered a son, with twenty-five-year-old Elizabeth Turner. Not one who could be accused of being a romantic, the story of their first meeting goes that she was brought to the house of James Toverys, on the pretence of a woman wishing to talk to her. Instead she was taken to a chamber where she was faced with four revenue officers, one being Lisle. They were left alone together, and got to know one another as best they could, the end result being a baby boy born in 1719. Lisle was ordered to pay 20s immediately and then 1*s* 2*d* per week for the child's upkeep. A further instalment of 50*s* was expected when he reached the age of ten to aid his apprenticeship.

Lisle's career started to take off in 1724 when he made his first seizure at Small Mouth in the mouth of Portland Harbour. By 1730 he was being referred to as Captain Lisle. This suggests that between 1724 and 1730, Lisle had been to sea, gaining the respect and experience required to be referred to as captain.

Lisle soon started to rise up through the ranks of the revenue service, becoming the supervisor for Weymouth. This position would have brought him into direct contact, or at least close contact, with the smugglers. He had a number of riding officers stationed along the coast and inland in Dorchester; Abbotsbury; Portland; Osmington; Langton; and Wyke. He also had companies of dragoons on call at Corfe Castle, Wareham, Dorchester and Weymouth.

But unlike Lisle, his riding officers were not as conscientious, thorough and hardworking. In fact, many of his officers were either too old to care or drunkards. This is illustrated by the story of one riding officer who rode his horse at speed into the sea telling all that he was going to ride this way to Bridport. He was brought ashore, taken home but died two days later.

In 1732 Warren Lisle settled into his new home in Weymouth on the corner of St Edmunds Street, the residence normally reserved for the collector of Weymouth, also earning and gaining a reputation for catching smugglers.

However, 1734 saw a change in Warren Lisle's career, when he bought the sloop *Walker* from the Crown. (This supports the idea that his 'missing' years had been spent at sea.) Taking on the vessel he was surprised how neglected and tired it was. Using his own money, he completely refitted and re-armed the vessel and then hired the vessel back to the crown and collector of Weymouth at a rate of 2*s* 6*d* per month per ton.

In 1737 he seized a Guernsey packet used to smuggle goods from the Channel Islands, once again on receipt of his share of the seizure he purchased the vessel from the Crown, renaming her the *Beehive*. She was eventually hired out to the collector of Weymouth and operated from Hengistbury Head in the east as far to the west as Start Point.

The year 1740 saw another progression in Warren Lisle's career when he was made surveyor of the sloops along the South Coast. The area of responsibility covered from Portsmouth down to Lands' End. As the surveyor of the sloops, Lisle would have been consulted in all aspects of catching and the prevention of the smugglers even down to the type of hardware to be used. Lisle's next move was to Exeter, but he didn't stay long, in 1745 he moved to Lyme Regis where, in 1751, he was elected mayor. He was elected to the office not just once but for a second and third term in the early 1760s.

Captain Lisle retired the *Beehive* as it was worn and tired, only to replace her in 1756 when he purchased the *Shaftsbury* which was stationed at Penzance. He later purchased the *Sherborne* which was stationed at Lyme Regis.

Another of Warren Lisle's activities was a war against corruption within the revenue service; he was used to look into and examine bad administration of customs matters at Plymouth and Penzance, resulting in both cases of the accused revenue officers been dismissed from the service for 'being in with the smugglers'.

In 1770 Warren Lisle and his wife returned to Weymouth, which as it so happened pleased his wife as she had inherited the Minterne and Clapcott estate and by 1780 they were living on a fine estate at Upwey near Weymouth.

In 1773 he resigned the post of searcher for Poole and Weymouth after fifty-seven years of service. He was replaced by his son, William. Six years later he then resigned as surveyor of the sloops. At the age of seventy-nine, he just wanted to be free from the constraints of the service and the abuse and as such wrote a number of reports directly to Lord Shelburne, the Home Secretary (the first home secretary in 1782) at the time, about the state of smuggling which was on the increase.

He never did fully let go and even in his later years he made a report on HMS *Orestes,* a prominent vessel in the battle of Mudeford in 1784.

Warren wrote to Lord Shelburne on 31 July 1782 outlining his reasons for retiring:

> Because I could serve no longer with honour or credit to myself for being connected to Lyme and having some interest there and choosing to exercise my own opinion and to give my vote agreeable to my own dictates, I thought it more prudent to quit that service which I and every other person in my predicament were threatened we should be dismissed from, if we dared speak against the interest of the fanes there.

In 1788 Warren Lisle died at the age of ninety-three. He was buried in the church of St Lawrence in Upwey. Lisle was a fine upstanding customs officer and searcher of customs at Weymouth from 1721–1773 and during his forty-year career was known to have been the 'utmost terror to the smugglers'.

The original Haven Inn, Mudeford Quay

The new Haven House Inn, Mudeford Quay

The cottages at the end of the Haven built to house the workers who dredged the harbour

Looking towards Avon Beach, the site of the Battle of Mudeford

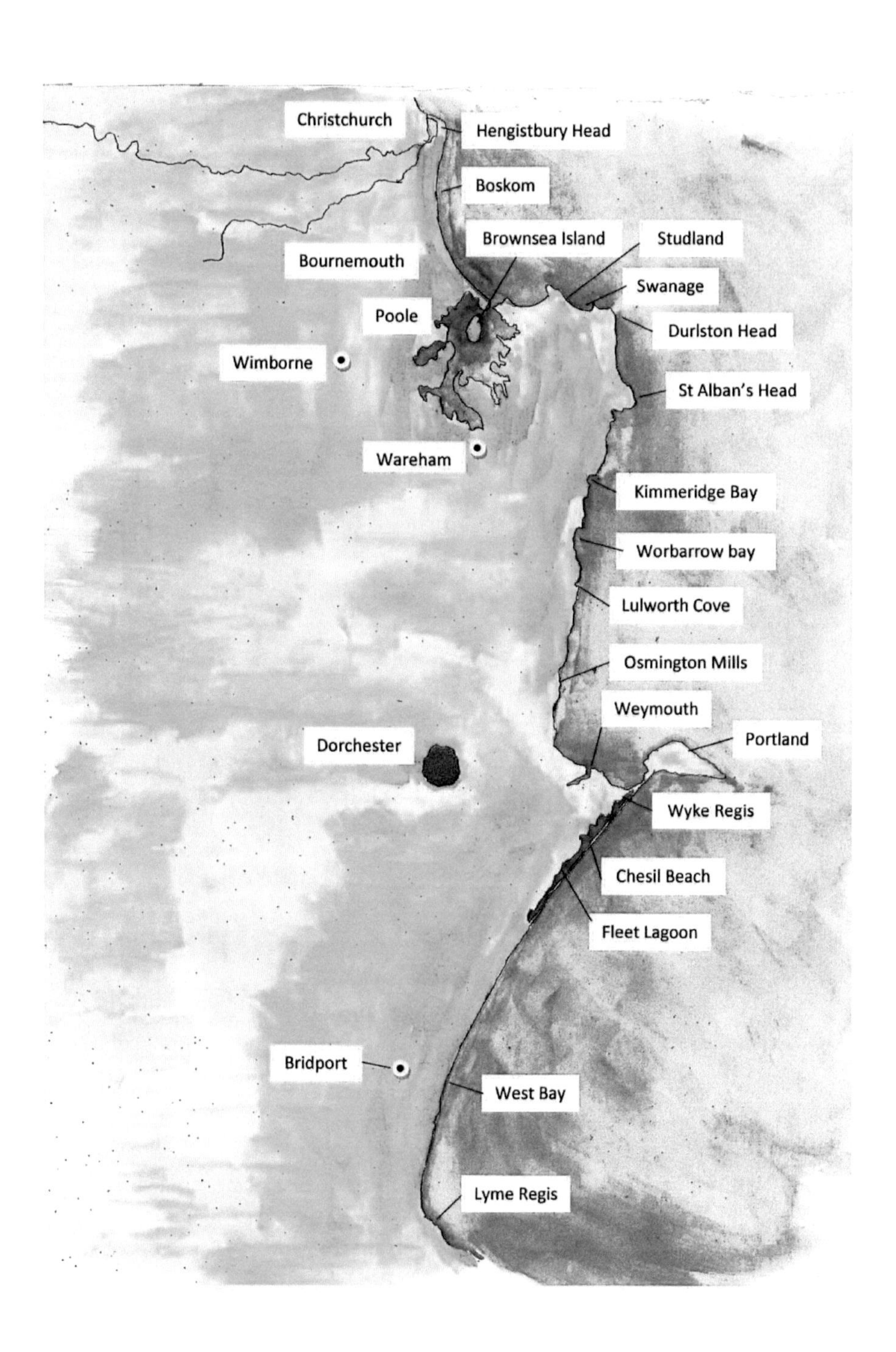
Christchurch
Hengistbury Head
Boskom
Brownsea Island
Studland
Bournemouth
Swanage
Poole
Durlston Head
Wimborne
St Alban's Head
Wareham
Kimmeridge Bay
Worbarrow bay
Lulworth Cove
Osmington Mills
Weymouth
Portland
Dorchester
Wyke Regis
Chesil Beach
Fleet Lagoon
Bridport
West Bay
Lyme Regis

4

Dorset Coastline: the landing places and hiding places

Christchurch is situated in the confluence of the River Stour and the River Avon, the result being that Christchurch became a trading port, a shelter and a safe mooring for the traveller that frequented the quay and haven. It is therefore natural that smugglers also took great advantage of the area and what the harbour had to offer.

The entrance to the harbour is a narrow difficult stretch of water and when the tide is running in or out is a very fast (on an ebb tide anything up to 8 knots) moving stretch of water, and potentially a very dangerous stretch of water. Christchurch Harbour is also subject to a double tide each day, which can vary between 2½–4½ft of water and due to the double tide and the two rivers that meet in the harbour, the harbour has a tendency to silt up resulting in the restriction of the size of the vessels able to enter it. In addition, due to the fast run through the entrance to the harbour the only way in to the harbour was to sail in on the incoming tide and leave on the outgoing tide.

Christchurch itself relied on the sea trade to survive. Coal and other commodities such as tea, vinegar, tallow, candles, butter and soap all came into the town from Portsmouth, Southampton, Lymington and Poole via the sea. There were at least three breweries in Christchurch and records showed that vessels would come into the quay and load up with beer which was then taken to Portsmouth. Abraham Pike (the custom man for the area) recorded this trade in his journals of 1803 and 1804. Although smugglers, such as John Streeter, imported illegally vast quantities of contraband, goods like gin, rum and brandy were imported through the port legally and under the carful watch of the customs officers Abraham Pike and his predecessor Joshua Stevens Jeans.

One of the landing places used by the smugglers was around the Haven, an area at the entrance to Christchurch Harbour. This is where the famous Haven Inn, run by Hannah Sellers stands. Hannah took over after her husband died in 1780, but she also ran the Ship in

Distress at Stanpit. The present Haven Inn is not the original one, the original can be found by looking west along the Haven to the old cottages at the end; a cottage with a set of steps leading up the front of the building now known as the Dutch House is the original Haven Inn.

The cottages standing on the end of the Haven were originally built to house the workers involved in the dredging of the harbour and River Stour in the seventeenth century. The whole surrounding area is made up of gravel and ironstone, an ideal landing place for the smugglers. Looking east towards Avon Beach is where the events which became known as the Battle of Mudeford were to unfold on one night in 1784, when William Allen a revenue officer lost his life. The story ends with a smuggler George Coombes being tried and hanged for his murder, even though it is said he did not fire the fatal shot that killed William Allen. Today the whole area is very different: the shingle beach has gone and been replaced with the Haven car park, built in the 1950s.

If you now look across the run to Mudeford Spit you will see a very old black building. This building is known as the Black House and is sited on Gervis Point. Today it is holiday flats but back when Hannah Sillers ran the Haven Inn its use was totally different. Unsure as to when it was built and by whom, though it may have been Dutch settlers who arrived in the sixteenth century, the ground floor was once a large open space used as a sail-loft and as a boat building shed. During the Napoleonic times it is said that the guinea boats were built here. It is rumoured that the building is black after a revenue officer set fire to the building in an attempt to smoke out the boat builders and smugglers so they could be arrested.

Christchurch was lucky enough, in around 1784, to have its own supervisor and four riding officers. The supervisor was a Joshua Stevens Jeans, who, it appears, was also a friend of the smugglers and as a result, did not go out of his way to stop their activities. The smugglers themselves would provide him with his official seizures, that way it would look as if he was doing his job and not give rise to suspicion. His fellow riding officers were William Nelson, John Bursey, Robert Reeks and a James Noyce, these officers would have been stationed along the coast.

Joshua Jeans was to be replaced by an Abraham Pike, a slightly more attentive officer. (*See* Chapter 3 for an insight into what it must have been like to be a riding officer at the turn of the nineteenth century). A report in 1782 from the Earl of Shelburne decided that it was not a good idea to employ local people as riding officers, since bribery and corruption were rife within the ranks of the officers. In the case of Joshua Jeans this turned out to be true.

The Haven Inn was not the only drinking den frequented by the smugglers of Christchurch. Leaving the Haven car park and heading along the road 'Stanpit' towards Christchurch you come to one of the most famous inns frequented by the smugglers, the Ship in Distress.

The landlady here was Hannah Sillers, also known as Mother Sillers. She became the protective angel to the smugglers and tales abound of her wearing a red cape to signal to the smugglers that it was safe for them to bring in their contraband.

Backing onto the inn in Mother Sellers' day was Stanpit Marsh, which is a stretch of low lying marshland extending for approximately 130 acres and lying just below the confluence of the River Stour and the River Avon. One of the most famous areas of the marsh was a channel that became known as 'Mother Sellers Channel'. Today, if you walk across the marsh from the car park just up from the inn you will find the channel. Spanning the channel is another bit of Christchurch's history, the prototype Bailey Bridge designed and built at the barracks in Barrack Road during the Second World War.

In Mother Sellers' day, Stanpit Marsh would have been a wild and a very dangerous place to cross, especially if you did not know the safest route. At the eastern end of the channel is a point called Speillers Point and today the channel is very wide and comes through an area known as Grimmery Marsh until it reaches the area where the Bailey Bridge has been built. After the bridge, the channel disappears into the reeds and peters out, silted up and is no longer navigable.

Once the channel would have gone all the way up to the back door of the Ship in Distress allowing the smugglers to move the cargo into the cellars of the inn, and stories tell of the tunnels under the inn which would allow the contraband to be moved away out of sight. Talking to the present landlady she tells me that when the extension was built no tunnels were found. Today Stanpit Marsh is a nature reserve and no longer the habitat of the smugglers but the hunting ground of the ornithologists and ramblers with cameras and binoculars and can easily be accessed from the public car park by the recreation ground near the

The Haven, Mudeford c.1900

The Black House, Mudeford Sandspit

Ye Olde George Inn, Castle Street, Christchurch

inn. Next door to the inn on the right is where it is believed that John Streeter had his tobacco factory.

As for other haunts of the smugglers there are Ye Olde Eight Bells in Church Street, now a Grade II listed building, dating from 1450. The name of the inn comes from Christchurch Priory Church which dominates the area, and particularly the Priory's peal. When the inn was in business the church had seven bells, unlike today where there are twelve. The name Eight Bells apparently was a joke along the lines of the nineteenth hole on a golf course. Sadly Ye Olde Eight Bells is no longer an inn; it served its last pint in 1907 and today is a gift shop.

There is an interesting smuggling story associated with this inn. A warning was given of revenue men coming to search the premises and the kegs were removed quickly, but on this occasion one keg was overlooked. A quick-minded woman noticed the keg and sat down on it and shaking out her long skirt covered the keg; she then proceeded to bathe her baby. The revenue men noticed she was busy and allowed her to carry on and nothing was found. There is also supposedly a tunnel which runs from the cellars of the inn out across to the Ship in Distress about a mile away.

On the corner of Castle Street and Christchurch High Street you will see another favourite haunt of the smugglers: Ye Olde George Inn, formerly the George and Dragon. The name was abbreviated to The George and then The George Hotel. The abbreviations misled the brewery to name the inn, Ye Olde George Inn after the Hanoverian King.

It was once the coach house for the Emerald Coach service, which would have stopped en route from Lymington and Poole. If you go into the courtyard from Castle Street, there are various stories on the walls of how the inn was used to house and transport prisoners to waiting ships at Poole quay ready to take them to the plantations in the Americas. The notices also point out where the cells supposedly used to be. There are also stories of tunnels that lead to various nearby buildings from the cellars of the inn.

Then there is the Ship Inn along the High Street, holder of the oldest current licence in Christchurch; and on the main Lyndhurst Road there is the Cat and Fiddle, and Chewton Glen; lastly, there is the Place Mill on the quay, all of these were drinking spots for the smugglers.

Walking back down Castle Street past Lloyds bank and over the first bridge into Bridge Street you will come across the residence of the revenue officer, Abraham Pike at No. 10 Bridge Street. From there he would plan his next move on the smugglers trying to outwit and capture them, going down to the Haven and the quay overseeing the loading and unloading of the many vessels that frequented the area. His true title was, *The Supervisor of Customs and Coast Waiter*. The 'coast waiter' meant that he would have had to oversee the loading and unloading of cargo from the ships that docked at the quay and Haven which would explain the many entries in his journals of visiting the quay and the Haven. In No. 10 Bridge Street there were cellars and it would have been here where seized goods would have been housed until taken to Poole warehouse.

Pike's job must have been very difficult as most of the town's folk were involved in one way or other with the smugglers. In the year of 1800 there would have been around 1,100 people living in the town, many involved with fishing for turbot, soles, whiting, mullet, herring, mackerel or salmon, which would not fetch a large amount of money, roughly 10*d* per lb. Then during the summer months, they would catch shrimps and prawns. Others would have worked in the breweries or in the fields as labourers while the women folk would knit silk or worsted stockings to be exported to Newfoundland along with gloves. There was also the fusee factory with Robert Cox who in 1790 began manufacturing chains in a factory on the High Street and by 1793 he had gained the monopoly for the manufacture of chains and employed forty to fifty children, making fusee chains for watch movements, and the average wage could be 6*s* or 7*s* a week, and at the time the rent could be as much as 30–40*s* a year. Then in 1845 William Hart opened a similar factory in Bargate which stayed open until the late 1890s when it was sold. The building is still there with its high windows.

This illustrates how poor many of these people would have been and why they engaged in smuggling activities to supplement their income, many acting as runners or landers. A lander could earn as much as 10*s* a night for helping unload the vessels and then moving the cargo off to a safe hiding place ashore. As virtually everybody within the town would have been involved with the illicit trade it meant they all would have something to lose if caught out and therefore nobody was likely to snitch on their neighbours or friends.

The Ship Inn, Christchurch High Street

Ye Olde Eight Bells, Church Street, Christchurch

The Red House Museum, Quay Road, Christchurch

Near Christchurch Priory is the old workhouse in Quay Road, just across the graveyard from the church, and this would have housed around 130 people. Today the old workhouse is the Red House Museum and on the outside wall can be found a blue plaque telling the story.

Another one of Christchurch's landmarks, but now long gone, was the barracks along Barrack Road. They were first erected in 1792 as a result of a report from the Commissioner of Military Enquiry. They served as a barracks for years after, eventually being demolished in 1996, with the land being used for housing. The old stable blocks were converted into flats and the guard house is now a beauty salon. Initially, it was only big enough to house a company of Light Dragoons and then later extended to house three troops of cavalry, or one of the Royal House Artillery. The barracks were originally built as an anti-invasion precaution rather than to combat the ever-rising threat from the smugglers, although they could be called on to assist the revenue officers as, and when, needed. As in many cases the revenue officers on their own would have been well outnumbered by the gangs of smugglers that could be assembled to unload a waiting vessel, and who would also have been armed and fully prepared to use their weapons.

There are many stories of how people used to help the smugglers. This particular tale involved one of the most prominent people in Christchurch: Dr Quartley, Mayor of Christchurch in 1836, 1837 and 1838. He lived on the thin strip of land between the River Stour and the Millstream. The story goes that one evening the doctor was called out to attend to an injured smuggler believed to have been shot in the back after an exchange with the revenue men. The following day the doctor found a keg of spirits outside on his front door step with a note attached saying, 'left here for the Doctors fees'. The doctor pulled the stopper and found it to be full of French brandy. Fifteen years later, the doctor was dining with an old friend, a Mr Mills at Bisterne Manor, and after dinner they all went for a row on the River Avon. The two boat crew were Mr Mill's gardeners and it turns out that one of the gardeners was the man the doctor had removed the slug from fifteen years previously.

The locals would go to any length to help the smugglers. They would help by providing muffled harness for wagons and horses, and this was done by greasing the wagons well and also by putting felt on the horses' shoes. Sometimes as revenue officers gave chase to the smugglers the locals would block the way with wagons or flocks of sheep. To hide the fact that the smugglers had passed a particular way, the muddy roads would have cattle driven down them and any tracks from the smugglers' wagons or horses would be obliterated, and then the hayricks and manure heaps would be used to hide the tubs. There is one story of a farmer coming out to the fields to find his hayricks had moved and had grown in size; on investigation he found kegs in the middle of them.

The smugglers of Christchurch would have been well-organised and willing, when landing a cargo; everything was organised and everything was in place: the horse and carts, the runners, and the landers or tub men, like a fully oiled machine, all knowing what was expected from each other.

The Grammar School at Christchurch was held in St Michael's Loft, over the Lady Chapel of the Priory Church and at the time the view was incredible across the harbour to Hengistbury Head and beyond. The students could look out and watch the procession of twenty or thirty wagons with an armed man sitting front and back and men on horseback, each with two to four tubs of spirits attached to their saddles, making their way along Hengistbury Head possibly with the revenue men looking on powerless to do anything, a handful of officers against a gang of smugglers, armed and dangerous numbering anything up to 200 men. Maybe the smugglers would leave a keg or two for the officers, who knows?

One of the many problems for the smugglers in Christchurch was the two rivers. In many respects they helped the smugglers in hiding and landing their cargoes, but the Stour and the Avon also needed to be crossed. Once the cargo had been landed and moved away inland the rivers became an obstacle to distribution. For example, the goods landed at Hengistbury Head would probably have been taken into the New Forest, and would have had to have been taken across the River Stour at Wick ferry (fording the river), or at Iford (across the bridge), and then on towards Bransgore.

We also find today that some of the routes and roads taken by the smugglers have been named either after them or for their activities. For example: Smugglers Lane in Highcliffe, and also in Wimborne,

The only remaining building, the old guardroom, at MVEE

Iford Bridge

Iford Bridge

Iford Bridge and the River Stour

Owls Road in Boscombe (I suspect after the Owlers – wool smugglers, Gulliver's Court in Wimborne (named after Isaac Gulliver) and Smugglers Wood Road in Christchurch. Beacon Drive in Christchurch is located not too far from the coast, and it was there that the smugglers signalled the ships at sea if it was safe to come in and land the cargo. Kimmeridge has Brandy Bay, well known for its smuggling activities.

Just outside Christchurch can be found yet another small hamlet known today as Iford, but in the nineteenth century it was called Iver and was located on the banks of River Stour. It was well known as a fording place, since the little 'eyelets' or 'islands' made crossing the river relatively easy. This small hamlet of a few cottages was the nearest place to the sea that could be safely crossed. It was fordable by horseback and even, in dryer times, one could have waded across.

Over the years bridges were built to cross the river. In those days they were regarded as a charity and were kept by the alms of those who used it and also by legacies (money left in a will). The wills of John Howkie and John Corbin can be found in Holdenhurst Church, dated 1560 and 1590 respectively, they detail the money left for the construction of Iver Bridge. The bridges would have been built across the river from one island to the next making the spans short between two and four arches.

Iford is the location of a tale that illustrates the dangers in dealing with smugglers. As reported in the *Salisbury and Winchester Journal* on 20 December 1762, a gang of eight smugglers (claiming to be press gang) broke into William Manuel's house and violently took away his son, Joseph. They dragged the poor boy from the house, across the heath towards Poole and onto the Decoy Pond House at Bournemouth. From there he was forced onto a smuggler's vessel and taken by force to Alderney where miraculously he managed to escape but not without been badly injured. This was all because the smugglers believed that William Manuel father had passed on information to the revenue men.

The actions of that day are said to be instigated by a more important smuggler from along this part of the coast, who hired the men to do his deed. The commissioners of customs in order to bring the men responsible to justice posted a reward of £50 for any information that would lead to a conviction.

Hengistbury Head, down the coast from Christchurch, is an area that has a long tradition of industry. Archaeological records suggest it was an ancient centre of metal working, using the local iron ore, the area's importance only declining during the Roman occupation since they preferred Wareham to Hengistbury Head.

One of the most impressive features of the area is the double dykes that protected the hill fort on the headland. These are believed to have stretched around the head and down to the sea, and when first built must have been quite spectacular. After hundreds of years of erosion and now heavily overgrown they are still impressive.

In the seventeenth and eighteenth century they were used not as a form of defence but as a hiding place by the smugglers. The double dykes reached right down to the sea and would provide cover for the smugglers while they waited quietly for the vessels to come in and land their cargo. They were a perfect place to hide wagons and horses and as such became one of the best landing places along the coast. The smugglers would hide their vessels behind the Needles, wait till the coast was clear then come in and land their cargoes. When the smuggler's vessel was coming into land their cargo at Hengistbury Head they would have been shown a blue light from the cliffs and then waited to be answered with a 'flink' via a spout lantern. If you were caught signalling a smuggler's vessel the punishment would be very severe.

The waters around this area are quite dangerous and knowledge of the double tides and shifting sands would have been a great advantage. With the double dykes reaching down to the sea and the transport to move the cargo away all hidden safely within the dykes, the unloading of the cargo would have been fast. This would have enabled the lander to give the order to move on and allow the procession of wagons carts and horses to leave via the double dykes, making their way up along what is now Broadway Avenue until they reached the gravel track (the old smuggler's track) on the right hand side of the road which today is on the edge of the Solent Mead Golf Course. They would then have crossed the current golf course and about half way across this area would have been the point the students at the grammar school in Christchurch Priory Church would have seen them wending their way along en route to Wick and across the River Stour towards the New Forest.

The Beach, Hengistbury Head, the Needles in the background

The Double Dykes, Hengistbury Head, where smugglers would hide

The village green at Wick

Wick Ferry across the Stour to Christchurch

Wick, located on the southern banks of the River Stour, would have been a small village that consisted of a few cottages built around the triangular village green, and strange as it might sound, there was no pub or a church within the village.

Bournemouth did not exist in the early days of the smugglers but was a desolate place of heath land and gorse or as it was known in those days' furze. The only building at the time, in what was then Bourne Bottom (where the River Bourne reached the sea), was called Decoy Pond House or Bourne House. It was located on Decoy Pond which is close to the current day war memorial by the Town Hall, unlike today where Coy Pond can be found further upstream. The area between the Middle and Alum chines (known as Allumin) also rough ground sparsely covered in gorse and heath, presented a perfect landing and hiding place for the smugglers. Often teams of packhorses would wait on the barren cliff tops for cargoes of illicit goods to arrive and to carry them away into the night.

The routes these smugglers took across the heath land became over the year's well-trodden paths and in the end would become the main routes throughout the town. In addition, routes out of the town which are today expensive residential areas would have been haunts for the smugglers. For example, Glenferness Avenue was once a lonely desolate place of barren heath land and just off the main road was Pug Hole which was a location where the smugglers would hide their wares. Dick Shepard in his book 'Ghosts of Bournemouth' mentions that in these areas maybe the ghosts of smugglers are still there guarding their contraband.

One of the most famous smugglers to land his last cargo of contraband by the mouth of the River Bourne near where Bournemouth Pier now stands was Isaac Gulliver. It is said that the line of wagons leaving the area was two miles long.

Another smuggler that used the Chines to smuggle goods in on regular basis was an Edward Beake. Described in the Poole Letter Book of 1777 as 'a very great smuggler' and had 'lately had great success'. A violent affray that occurred on Bourne Heath in 1770 saw Edward being identified as one of the nineteen smugglers involved. The story goes that the smugglers got upset when four customs officers from Christchurch seized a wagon containing sixty tubs of spirits on a spot on the heath called White Pits. One of the officers, Jasper Bursey, was thrown over the reeves of the wagon and onto the casks on the ground. With that the smugglers escaped only to be chased by Jasper Bursey who managed to shoot one of the smugglers' horses. The smugglers, with the aid of their colleagues, confined the officers for two hours. The officers eventually reached the beach where they found Edward Beake and a further twenty-five casks. Edward struck Jasper, but on the other hand offered Jasper's colleagues a share in his bread and cheese dinner.

Edward Beake had many accomplices: his brother-in-law William Harris who lived at Decoy Pond House, another brother-in-law from Christchurch, George Stewart, who apparently spent time in Dorchester Gaol in 1773 and another relative Robert Newman. There was John Dury a labourer from Pokesdown and William Frampton Beake's 'constant assistant'. Edward Beake's name carries on appearing within the Poole Letter Book over the next few years.

To conclude the story of Jasper Bursey, the riding officer who tried on that fateful night in 1770 to apprehend Edward Beake, he met his end at the hands of two smugglers. After being woken one morning by two smugglers knocking on his door claiming they had information on a large quantity of smuggled goods and would take him to it, Jasper got dressed and went downstairs to the front door. The two smugglers dashed Jasper's brains out killing him where he stood.

There were also many success stories of the seizure of cargoes by the revenue officers. For example, in March 1821, 130 tubs of foreign spirits were picked up on the beach and lodged in the warehouse at Poole. On 12 October 1821 officers stationed at Bournemouth seized forty-two tubs of brandy and other foreign spirits, and lodged them at the warehouse at Poole.

The coast and cliff tops along what would become Bournemouth sea front would have seen much smuggling activity throughout the years and as such the smugglers learned many new ways of being able to fool and trick the revenue officers into believing that a landing was been arranged in one place, only in fact for it to be carried in a completely different place. For example, false lights would have been hung along the coast purely to act as a decoy for the excise men and whilst they would be chasing a false lead the smugglers would quickly land their cargo somewhere else and be off into the night. If the revenue officers by chance did get it right, the smugglers would then

Gulliver's Tavern, Kinson

Redhill Common

Redhill Common

Smugglers' routes, Redhill Common

'flash off' the vessels using a flint warning them of revenue officers in the area. The diaries of the first Earl of Malmesbury, state that 'a considerable contraband trade was carried along these coasts and the cargoes carried along these coast would be hidden/concealed within the furze bushes that extended from Ringwood to Poole and into the new forest for about 30 miles'.

Moving out of Bournemouth and into the smaller outlying villages, we come across Kinson, or as it was known in those days Kingston. This area was known to be a smugglers' haven, and was the home of one of the most famous smugglers of his time, Isaac Gulliver. There is one incident which I think warrants a mention. The *Evening Echo* on 16 May 1987 carried the headline, 'When Kinson took on the Kings Men'. It tells the story of when custom officers and thirty-seven men in the service of King George III rode into Kingston on search of contraband, supposedly hidden within a barn. If Isaac Gulliver was involved in this the barn may have been at Pitts Farm. One hundred country folk on foot and horseback armed with pistols, cutlasses, cudgels and pitchforks engaged the custom officers. The result of this fierce battle saw twenty-seven of the men confined to sick quarters under the surgeon. The gang leaders were identified as John Dolman, John King, William Russell, John and William Butler, John Gillingham, John Saunders, Robert Brine and the innkeeper' wife Hannah Potter, the Inn being the Dolphin Inn, now known as Gulliver's Tavern.

Gulliver's Tavern was built in 1750 and is now a Grade II listed building, but was it once one of Isaac Gulliver's properties? It may well have been. The landlord at the time was a John Potter and his wife Hannah Potter both knew Isaac Gulliver well. They knew each other from when Isaac Gulliver brought Pitts Farm from a Mary Barnes in 1775 as John and Hannah were tenants of Mary Barnes. Even more interesting is the inn on the opposite side of the road – the Royal Oak. When it was demolished, secret underground passageways were discovered on the land, not surprising given the area was apparently known as 'Brandy ground'.

Moving eastwards we find Redhill which was just a small hamlet of a few scattered mud cottages among an area of open heath in the 1700/1800s. The gorse and furze would have no doubt also offered good protection for activities of the day and also a good hiding place for the illicit cargoes that would have made their way across the heath. The residents of these cottages would also have been sympathisers of the smugglers as the stories of the time show.

One cottage on the northern edge of the common had its own little hiding place. The walls of these cottages would have been around two feet thick and would have been made of mud and straw. When two cottages were demolished to make way for the road that now cuts through the common, one cottage was found to have a hiding place within the wall of the cottage under the window sill. It must have been a good hiding place as one day when the lady of the cottage was home on her own, the revenue men paid her a visit and searched the cottage for smuggled goods. Finding nothing they left, but all the time in this particular hiding place was a number of kegs of brandy.

The false tomb at St Andrews Church, Kinson

Other cottages within this small hamlet also had their own special hiding places that no one else knew about including their neighbours, for example stacks of turf and furze next to the cottages was not what it seemed. Hidden within these stacks could be found smuggled goods such as kegs of brandy.

Redhill Common seems to be one of the routes taken by the smugglers to get to Kinson and maybe St Andrews church and the churchyard where the goods would have been hidden within the tower of the church or the false tomb where the sides would open to reveal a very good and safe hiding place. This was one of the best hiding places as officers did not want to be seen to disturb and desecrate a tomb, or even enter the church and violate a sacred building.

On the edge of the East Dorset border is a small town of Verwood or as it was known in 1826 Fairwood. They too had their own smuggler in Daniel Sins. He shows the extent smugglers would go to protect and retrieve their illicit cargoes.

Sins had eleven casks of spirits at his home and on one occasion the revenue officers from Cranborne decided to pay him a visit and seized the goods. Knowing what was going on, Sins mounted his horse and rode at full speed to the Fleur De Lys Inn in Cranborne. Entering the bar, he sat down quietly next to the chimney and waited with his pipe and a drink. He did not have to wait long before somebody walked in who was full of the events of the day and what had been discovered. Sins then soon found out where the eleven casks of liquor had been stored, which happened to be the home of the excise officer.

With this information he drank up and left the inn and with the help of a few friends made plans on how they could recover the casks. The party gathered with horses and carts at midnight near Cranborne. As it was dark and they did not want to make any mistakes their guide went ahead, entered Cranborne and marked the excise officer's house with white chalk. The gang entered Cranborne, beat the front door down with a sledge hammer and then started loading the cart and horses with the casks, whilst another looked on holding a pistol and threatening to blow out the excise officer's brains if anybody tried to stop them. Once the carts were fully loaded and secure and with an armed outrider front and back of the carts they galloped off into the night.

The paper and reports described them as ruffians, but as the Hawkhurst gang pointed out when they raided the warehouse in Poole one evening 'they only came for what was theirs'.

Sins met his end one day when he fell from his horse in 1826 at the age of sixty-seven.

Now further along the coast past Poole, Studland and Old Harry's Rock is the small town of Swanage. This place produces an interesting tale and refers to a quarryman who lived within 'Swanage' and by chance had a custom officer as a neighbour. The quarryman had trained his horse to make his way home on his own, normally carrying contraband smuggled ashore. On one occasion, when the quarryman was going about his smuggling activities, he loaded his horses with tubs and sent him on his way home. However, the horse did not go home but instead decided to go to his next door neighbour, the customs officer. As the horse approached the cottage the sound of the horse's hooves on the cobbles outside made the customs officer get up to investigate and on opening the door he was met by a horse carrying a cargo of tubs, which he seized and then sent the horse on his way head held low with shame. This story cannot be confirmed or denied but it still amusing.

Moving along the Jurassic coast you come to Durlstone Head once used by the smugglers to land and move the cargoes without being seen or detected. The quarries and surrounding caves were used as hiding places, and at the end of each day the goods would have been carried away hidden within the rush baskets which they carried back and forth each day from work. One hiding place used was the hollowed out blocks of rock which when full would be covered with smaller debris to conceal the goods. The revenue men when doing an inspection would have been told that these smaller pieces of marble were unsaleable and as such there was no call for them.

On Durlstone Head on the south-east corner of the Isle of Purbeck a cave hidden behind a rock that could easily be removed was found by a coast guard's dog; the cave was used by the smugglers to hide their contraband. Further along the coast are Tilly Whim caves, a limestone quarry worked during the eighteenth century. The origin of the name Tilly Whim deserves explanation: Tilly - a former quarryman; and Whim - a primitive form of crane used to lower the blocks into waiting boats. As the demand for the limestone slowed down, instead of working the quarry, the smugglers started to use the caves to store contraband. The tunnels would have extended many feet inland and had interconnecting tunnels and shafts. As long as the smugglers knew where they were going they could land and move the cargoes inland undetected. The caves have been closed to the public since 1976 due to a rock fall; the only inhabitants now are bats and various nesting birds.

Tilly Whim Caves, Isle of Purbeck

Further down the Jurassic coast is Lulworth Cove, a beautiful and picturesque spot and another good landing and hiding place for the smugglers. It is a fully enclosed cove, sheltered on all sides by the cliffs and as such a no better place for sinking the odd cargo or two as long as the smugglers sank the goods properly, unlike in 1717 when a keg floated to the surface and was instantly seized by the customs officers.

Lulworth Cove has also seen its own share of action between the revenue men and the smugglers, as in 1719 when a gang of smugglers was stopped near the cove trying to run a cargo of brandy and wine. A battle ensued which lasted around twelve hours, each side armed with swords, flails and clubs. Realising that they may not get away with the full cargo they kept some of the barrels with them, other gang members made off with some, and they abandoned the rest to the locals.

One local, Charles Weeks, managed to get one over on the revenue officers by purchasing from the public auctions seized cargoes and then mixing them with smuggled goods. If he was stopped he could produce the paper work that showed the cargo was legal and if he was detected he would just threaten the revenue officers with litigation, not something the customs men could easily afford on their wages, so they would let him go on his way.

Then there was the incident in 1825 when two preventative men were caught by a large gang of sixty to seventy smugglers. The smugglers relieved the officers of their swords and pistols and detained them, holding their heads over a cliff with the threat of been thrown over if they resisted, which of course they did not. They were then allowed to look on whilst a crop of 100 casks was brought ashore and taken away. The officers were tied up and left in a field to be found in the morning. At least they did not meet with the same ending as some of their fellow officers who had been thrown from the cliffs and washed away by the sea.

Much of the goods landed at Lulworth Cove would have made their way through Wool and passed through the hands of Tom Lucas, a man not to be crossed. He would look after the goods and then organise the movement and storage of the goods. Eventually Lucas was caught and arrested by the Bow Street Runners, because knowing his reputation they did not want to take any chances.

Another part of the Jurassic Coast used by the smugglers for landing

Entrance to Poole Harbour

Swanage

Purbeck cliffs and Old Harry

Lulworth Cove

their contraband was Kimmeridge Bay and the neighbouring Brandy Bay and Warbarrow Bay. Arish Mell beach located in the centre of Kimmeridge Bay was used to the familiar sight of a smuggling vessel been signalled to say it was safe to come ashore and land their cargo, as in 1719 at Warbarrow Bay when one of the biggest landings of contraband goods took place when five luggers all landed their cargoes at the same time.

There is a ghostly tale of the legend of Warbarrow Bay where the hog back of the hilly spine of the Purbecks plunges 550ft to the sea. The story tells of a solitary smuggler who was startled by a group of revenue officers at the far end of the long, lonely beach. Being unfamiliar with the area and not knowing where he was going, he ran along the beach until faced with a sheer cliff. Unable to climb the cliff and finding himself trapped, he turned to the sea, where in the pitch darkness he met his end by stoning. It is said that his gasping and screams and the splashing caused by the convulsions of his body can still be heard at the waning of the moon.

Another place worthy of a mention is Dancing Ledge, located further along the coast south-west of Swanage. It is an area of flat rock at the base of a small cliff. The name Dancing Ledge derives from the size of stone cut from here was the same size as a ballroom dance floor. Cut stone cut was transported by sea and around the coast to form part of Ramsgate Harbour. Being so flat the smugglers could land the cargo easily and once landed take it over the hill to Spyways Farm and from there move it onto more permanent places. One such space was under the roof in Langton Matravers Church, until one day during the Sunday service the roof collapsed onto the congregation below due to the weight of so many kegs.

Chesil Beach was another good place to land smuggled cargo. On the other side of the beach from the sea is a lagoon called the Fleet Lagoon. This was an excellent place to sink a cargo in the sheltered and protected water ready to be collected when the coast was clear. Chesil Beach itself stretches from Burton Bradstock down to Portland, a distance of around 17 miles varying in width from 36–200m and to a height of 5–14m. A good smuggler landing his cargo at night could, just by picking up the pebbles on the beach and checking their size, tell roughly where he was on the stretch of beach.

At the Portland end of Chesil Beach can be found Smugglers Cove.

Chesil Beach is open to the elements and the sea does hit this part of the coast hard and has been known to reduce vessels to no more than driftwood and taking their crews to the bottom with them. To demonstrate the power of the sea on one occasion a 500-ton vessel was lifted bodily up and deposited in the Fleet Lagoon.

Then there are the smugglers of Wyke, a small fishing village, and William Lewis who met his end in 1822 from a shot from the *Pigmy* schooner, a revenue cutter.

The Ship Inn in Wyke, which stood in Shrubbery Lane, appears to be the local centre for the smugglers and was run by a once mariner who when married decided to settle down and give up the sea life. The inn's cellars were large and open and as normal there are stories of secret passageways leading away to the fields on the foreshore. A more sinister and dark side of the town is Red Lane named as such after the pitched battles between the revenue officers and the smugglers, resulting the road flowing red from their blood.

Bridport was the centre for rope making, a place of high employment and, in fact, for the time a place of high wages, so much so that the people of Bridport did not have to resort to smuggling. However, one mile away is West Bay formerly known as Bridport Harbour. This has been the location of a harbour since 1385 and has gone through many changes up to the present-day. Being such a busy little port it had its own customs officer who more than likely spent his whole time rummaging through the hundreds of ships entering and leaving the harbour looking for smuggled goods.

The town of Bridport does appear within Dorchester Gaol records and as a town that was so wealthy from the rope manufacture it is strange to see so many entries especially featuring women. One, a Charlotte Drake, was charged with assaulting and obstructing an excise officer but the records show she was bailed for the crime, whilst others were charged with smuggling and either fined or spent a short time within the Dorchester Gaol.

A short distance down the coast along the A35 is Chideock, and turning off the A35 you soon arrive at Seatown. This was another centre for the smugglers, with high cliffs to the east and west. Golden Cap on the western side rises to around 619ft above sea level and was used by the smugglers as a lookout and signal station.

Warbarrow Bay

Warbarrow Bay

Dancing Ledge.
Notice the track marks worn into the rock face

Dancing Ledge

Chesil Beach and Fleet Lagoon

Chesil Beach

West Bay, originally called Bridport Harbour

Seatown

Within this area the smuggling was controlled by 'the Colonel', who he was and where he came from are unknown but, it is said that he was a local gent and more than likely one with military training. He controlled and ran the smuggling from Seatown to Charmouth mainly landing his cargoes on beaches at Cain's Folly at Stanton and also at Gabriel's Mouth being a natural gully lying not far from Golden Cap and the only access to the cliff top between Seatown and Charmouth.

The Colonel preferred to use packhorses to move the cargo rather than store the cargo locally. To dispose of the contraband, he would take it inland along and through Marshwood Vale, along the River Chare and then onto the market towns of Beaminster and Broadwindsor. Here goods would be dropped off; some of his customers would have been the gentry and as such he would have delivered his cargo at the manor houses along the way. The Colonel then would have moved into Somerset, calling at Crewkerne, Chard and Yeovil dropping off the cargo as he went.

One thing the smugglers would do within this area was to leave landmarks on the highest points to aid the smugglers when landing their cargoes. This would also help them to identify where they were along the coast. As you drive through Bridport on the A35, on the hilltops around you can see three trees; apparently the smugglers would plant the trees on the hilltops as markers towards their favourite landing places. A copse of trees can be found on the hilltops at Charmouth and Seatown and many other places along this part of the coast. Burton Bradstock and Eggardon Hill are just other examples where the area was got ready for a plantation by Isaac Gulliver and trees planted only to be cut down by the revenue officers.

Lyme Regis on the edge of the Dorset and Devon border is a town with a long and distinguished reputation for smuggling. It was frequented by many famous smugglers, including Isaac Gulliver and his White Wigs who in 1776 unloaded a cargo right in front of the customs house then moved the cargo off through Whitchurch, Cononilorum, to Crewkerne and then onto Bristol.

Lyme Regis is also famous for the supposed birth place of William Lisle, one of the most conscientious and vigilant customs officers of his time. Reports of smuggling within Lyme Regis dates back to the sixteenth century when the smugglers were suspected of smuggling bullion out of the country to such a point that a Ralph Lane, in 1576, was dispatched to the town with a warrant to search the vessels. This caused an upset and as a result the warrant was destroyed and Ralph's deputy was thrown overboard.

How was the smuggled cargo moved around and hidden?

Movement and hiding of the illicit cargoes also became an art in its self with very complex and well-built brick lined tunnels. Some of these would have been so large that a man would be able to stand up, though in some you would have had to crawl along. The idea of the tunnels was to move the cargoes from one place to the next without been detected. There are many stories of supposed locations of these tunnels and in some cases they have even been found.

When work was being carried out in Poole, workmen removed a manhole cover outside the Aquarium and tourist office to reveal a well-built tunnel fully lined with bricks; the route the tunnel took was apparently along the alley adjacent to Canute House, across Strand Street and into the High Street where it would once have led into the cellar of a smugglers inn. Apparently Canute House had a cellar which connected into the smugglers' culvert and from there when the culvert was flooded the smugglers would float a rope down to the quay and then attach a keg to the end and pull the keg through the tunnels and into the cellars. Their work was made much easier when the tunnels were flooded.

Revenue men became wise to these antics and, one day, set a trap. When the smugglers floated a rope down through the tunnels waiting for them at the other end was a revenue officer who attached a tub onto the end of the rope with the message 'The end is nigh' chalked on it. He then gave a tug on the rope, a signal telling the smugglers on the other end to pull it through. When the smugglers at the end of the rope read the message they knew a trap was set and ready to be sprung shut, and sure enough the revenue officers caught them.

Another interesting area reputedly to be riddled with tunnels is Kinson. When the work started at the rear of the St Andrews Church to clear the land to make way for a new classroom and church hall, approximately 5ft underground, and running along the path of the churchyard, a 3ft 6in-diameter brick-lined tunnel was uncovered by the foreman a David Lockyer of B.A. Riketts. As you travel down through the tunnels shafts of light would shine from above down through the air vents and as you approached a building the tunnels opened out into a chamber. These tunnels reputedly ran from here all the way to Christchurch and Poole. Speculation is and always has been rife about these tunnels. Were they really smugglers tunnels or just water culverts and drains? And were the chambers just ice houses?

The ingenuity of the smugglers to move their cargoes was incredible and one amusing method was to stage a mock funeral to help move the goods. By placing the illicit cargo into the coffin and then with a good supply of mourners, horses with black plumes, the funeral party would walk slowly through the villages. Once clear of the village they would go into a full gallop, and they kept doing that until they reached their destination.

To keep the prying eyes away from the smuggler's hiding places, the smugglers would devise and concoct ghostly stories and in some cases act them out. These stories have been carried down through the years and become part of local legends with people not realising the origins may be the vivid imagination of a smuggler.

Smugglers were also ingenious in finding their own hiding places and many of these were so good no one would ever suspect they existed. One such hiding pace was found in 1936 when work was being carried out on the Old Crown Hotel on the corner of Wimborne Square and East Borough. From the public bar there was a room called the Ante room where old ladies would sit and knit. In this room was a large fireplace; you could walk into the fire place, up some steps onto a platform then down some more steps into another room, a hidden room. When the fire was lit the entrance would have been disguised. The room has reputedly been used by smugglers and highway men.

5

The Forces against the Smugglers and the Punishments if Caught

The fight against smuggling started in earnest in 1695 when approximately 300 riding officers were appointed by the Crown. These officers were initially brought in to stop the smuggling of wool out of the country by the then known 'owlers' and if caught the penalty at the time for 'owling' was very severe indeed – death. However, the introduction of a new import and export tax provided the riding offers with a new role, that of duty collection.

A milestone came in 1671 when the collection of the duty reverted back to the crown. Prior to this date the collection was passed out to syndicates of business men who would have to pay a rent to the crown and then whatever they collected they would have kept. Certain ports were only allowed to export the wool and these were called 'Staple ports' and Poole was one of them (allocated the status in 1433). But the merchants found it much easier and more profitable to load their ships at night in one of the many lonely creeks and inlets along the Dorset coast, and this was the real start of the smuggling trade or as they were also known 'free traders'.

Life for smugglers at this time was comparatively easy as there were not too many customs officers patrolling the coastline, the area they had to cover was generally rather large and their only means of transport was their horse. As an example, William Lowe's area of patrol was from West Dorset through to Hampshire and then onto Sussex an area impossible to cover with any great success. But help was at hand in the form of the revenue cutters which were introduced in the fourteenth century. However, they only covered the estuaries and the ports leaving great areas of the coastline still unprotected and the smugglers took good advantage of this, landing and running large quantities of contraband with ease and undisturbed. But this was soon to change as the number of revenue officers increased and the areas to patrol became smaller and easier to handle. In response the smugglers altered their methods and started taking on board smaller quantities of contraband allowing the smugglers to move quickly, land the cargo and reload it onto a waiting horse or wagon and then move off with speed before been detected.

In 1713 the riding officers were given a small amount of power and the assistance of the local Dragoons who were stationed along the coast and could be called on as and when required. To show that the Dragoons were being sent to assist the officers in the fight against smuggling within the Weymouth Letter Book there is an entry for 24 December 1737 where they acknowledge the receipt of a letter informing the commissioners they were in want of soldiers to be stationed at several places around the area to assist with the officers in the prevention of smuggling. It appears that they succeeded in getting ten Dragoons who would be quartered at Corfe Castle, Wareham, Dorchester and Weymouth to be called on as and when required.

As time went by, smuggling increased within the area putting so much pressure on the riding officers that on 28 September 1717 a request was put forward for three more riding officers, one for Cerne Abbas, one for Dorchester and one for Piddletown. The Weymouth Letter Book shows an entry for 9 November 1717 for the appointment of only one new riding officer a John Oldfield who was to be stationed at Dorchester. His area would have been from East Lulworth to West Abbotsbury. The life of a riding officer was such that the request was for an unmarried man, to be hardy and also be well acquainted with the area.

As most of the officers were single men, local girls were forbidden from seeing them because generally, the girls' families were involved in the smuggling trade. But this did not stop some of the younger officers, and the result would have been the poor girls ending up in trouble, as happened in 1722. Four young girls appeared in court testifying that the customs officers had got them pregnant. John Pinney, a Tidewaiter, seems to be a rather busy officer but not at catching smugglers! He had fathered two children within a few months, one to a nineteen-year-old neighbour of his, a girl called Grace Paul, and the second to twenty-four-year old Hannah Poole. Other officers also fathered illegitimate children and had to face the consequences, such as Samuel Butcher who also found he had fathered a baby girl with Mary Luce.

The riding officers and supervisors had to keep an exact journal setting forth each day's duties and to be precise in what they observed.

These journals would be inspected by their supervisor and then compared with other riding officers. If the accounts failed to match, then an investigation would occur. For example, Mr Robert Henly is mentioned in the Weymouth Letter Book on 19 June 1736 for irregularities in his journals. The point was that within his journals he mentions that the weather was 'foggy' but when compared with other journals and questioning of other riding officers there is no mention that the weather was foggy, showing that Mr Robert Henly was not surveying his area. Was he being paid by the smugglers to stay away whilst they went about their business? This we cannot know, but only surmise.

The riding officer was not the only enemy of the smugglers; there was also a large team of custom officers. Each port would have its own custom house. Poole Custom House is situated on the quay and was built on the site of the Elizabethan building which was destroyed in 1815. The present building was built in the Georgian style and modelled on the Guildhall in Market Street. Seized contraband would have been brought here and housed under lock and key till it could be destroyed or sold at a public auction. Residing here was the Controller of Customs; all other officers would answer to him. Then there was the Deputy Comptroller, an accountant, who would oversee and check the accounts of the Collector of Customs and then present them to the Comptroller General.

The surveyors were the workers who would face the smugglers and associated dangers. They would board the vessels, rummage through the ship searching for hidden goods and check the cargo against the ships manifesto. Surveyors would be split into Tide Surveyors who would inspect the vessels anchored off shore and Land Surveyors who would inspect the vessels at the quay side. There would have been a Coast Waiter and a Land Waiter who would have had a Searcher for exports and a Weigher for imports. As the name suggests he would weigh each item on the dock side as it was taken off the vessels and check it against the ship's manifesto.

Then there was a Tidesman who was responsible for the custom boat along with the Sitter (coxswain) and six oarsmen who manned the vessel, stationed at each port, and could also be called on at any point to act as a Watcher - keeping watch on the vessels whilst they were been unloaded.

Things must have been pretty bad and dangerous as on 3 December 1770, Robert Penny, the Tide Surveyor put in a request for a chest of small arms for the defence of himself and the six Tidesmen against the outrages of the smugglers which were very prolific at this time and also to persuade 'people or persons who are liable to perform quarantine to comply with His Majesty's order in council'.

By 1809 a uniformed customs waterguard was put forward. He was commonly known as the 'Preventative Waterguard' (also known as the 'Preventative Boat Service'). This arm of the service complimented the shore-based riding officers and they used to work together and collaborate to catch the smugglers. Initially based in watchtowers along the coast, the coastal waters would be patrolled through the night in the revenue cutters which came under admiralty control from 1816.

In 1821 a committee of enquiry examined all aspects of the custom service and looked at the 'Preventative Waterguard' service. Realising and understanding how important a force against the smugglers this was, it recommended that the force came under the control of the Board of Customs along with the riding officers and revenue cutters, so on 15 January 1822 the Treasury accepted this and a new force against the smugglers was born - 'The Coastguard Service'. This service was also instructed to take responsibility for wrecks and ensure the security of the vessel's cargo from looters. The boatmen were also trained in the art of saving lives. The riding officers stayed independent until they were amalgamated into an arm of the Customs and Excise in 1909; the organisation then operated until 1972 when the organisation was abolished and the duties were passed to the officers of HM Customs.

In 1816, as one of the methods to stop the revenue men being too friendly with the locals and the smugglers, it was decided to move the Boatmen around and away from their home town. For example, the boatman from Cowes ended up at Swansea. These men would not always be welcome in these new towns and they found it hard to find any accommodation for themselves and their families. To overcome this, the watchtowers were built in prominent positions on the coast with accommodation attached to them; this was the start of the coastguard houses.

The years that followed started to see the demise of smuggling as the navy took over the revenue cutters from around 1816, changing their tactics in the fight against the smugglers. Instead of blockading the French coast they decided to blockade the English coast, with great success. Statistics show there was a surge in seizures along the coast and within territorial waters which must have really hurt the pocket of the smugglers and their financiers. The Waterguard were further divided into thirty-one districts and these were further divided into 140 stations each managed by a Chief Officer (Sitter) Senior Boatman. Also the Admiralty appointed Revenue Commanders who were drawn from many Naval Lieutenants.

A further two measures saw the end of smuggling as we knew it in 1831: the Coast Guard service became a fully-fledged service and in 1848 the Corn Law Acts saw 450 items that were previously dutiable removed from the statue book. Overnight the smuggling trade was no longer profitable. Although smuggling continued, it was not to the same degree.

The smugglers all knew their trade well, they were very well organised, also they knew what would await them if they were caught, but the rewards for smuggling outweighed the risks. If they were caught, then often they became heroes and in some case their exploits would be told in song or poems for example Rudyard Kipling from Burwash wrote a poem about the smugglers:

'The Smugglers Song'

If you wake at midnight, and hear a horse's feet, don't go drawing back the blind, or looking in the street, Them that asks no questions isn't told a lie. Watch the wall, my darling, while the Gentlemen go by!

Five-and-twenty ponies, Trotting through the dark - Brandy for the Parson, 'Baccy for the Clerk; Laces for a lady; letters for a spy, And watch the wall, my darling, while the Gentlemen go by!

Running round the woodlump if you chance to find Little barrels, roped and tarred, all full of brandy-wine; Don't you shout to come and look, nor take 'em for your play; Put the brushwood back again, - and they'll be gone next day! If you see the stable-door setting open wide; If you see a tired horse lying down inside; If your mother mends a coat cut about and tore; If the lining's wet and warm – don't you ask no more!

If you meet King George's men, dressed in blue and red, You be careful what you say, and mindful what is said. If they call you 'pretty maid', and chuck you 'neath the chin, Don't you tell where no one is, nor yet where no one's been!

Knocks and footsteps round the house - whistles after dark –You've no call for running out till the house-dogs bark. Trusty's here, and Pincher's here, and see how dumb they lie -They don't fret to follow when the Gentlemen go by!

If you do as you've been told, likely there's a chance You'll be give a dainty doll, all the way from France, With a cap of Valenciennes, and a velvet hood -A present from the Gentlemen, along o' being good!

Five-and-twenty ponies, Trotting through the dark -Brandy for the Parson, 'Baccy for the Clerk. Them that asks no questions isn't told a lie Watch the wall, my darling, while the Gentlemen go by.

Impressments into His Majesty's Navy

In 1818, four known smugglers escaped from Poole Gaol, they were: John Barlett of Weymouth, Robert Comben, William Comben and George Way. The commissioners were keen to recapture them, posting a reward of £50. The escapees faced being impressed into the navy as punishment for their crimes.

The navy liked smugglers as they were usually very good sailors and during the Napoleonic Wars no sailor was safe from been impressed into the navy. Even the customs men were not safe, and to assist in the protection of the mariners joining a revenue cutter they would be furnished with written 'protection' which they had to carry with them at all times, even when off duty. An example of this was a John White. In 1808 he was a member of the crew of a revenue cutter that patrolled Christchurch Bay and surrounding area and he was issued with a Protection Parchment; this also carried a description of John White ensuring the Protection Parchment did not fall into the wrong hands.

It read as follows:

Custom House, London

16 February 1808

1808

Protection Customs

By the Commissioners for managing and causing to be levied and collected His Majesty's Customs

We do hereby certify that 'John White' whose age and description is at the foot hereof is employed as a mariner on Board the Rose cutter.

W. Warne, Johnson Commander, in the service of his Majesty's Customs

J. Willis J. Hurst

J, Munro J.G.Luttrell

Twenty Years of age, Five Feet four inches high, Brown complexion, short brown hair

This very important document very legal looking and important words like 'Protection' would be printed in red whilst the rest would be printed in black. Without this document life could easily change for John and not for the better.

As for the smugglers they took huge risks in being caught and impressed into the navy as they would not have a protection certificates. This was not good for the smugglers but even worse for their families who were left behind; all financial support would be gone for many years and who's to say they would even ever come home. Those impressed into the navy could not expect any special treatment; in fact, they received the opposite - a harsh and brutal life would await them controlled by the lash and noose. At home the smugglers wives and families could find themselves seeking parish relief and in those days you could only get help from the parish of your birth. A not uncommon case is reported where a 19-year-old smuggler's widow who was in debt, starving and in rags, shoplifted to feed herself only to be caught and sentenced to death. She was taken to the gallows still with her baby at her breast.

The archives at Poole show a number of examples of those impressed into the navy under the act - 47 Geo 3 Ch 66 Sect 15:

> Poole – 14 August 1816, John Galton and Timothy Ellis, both impressed into the navy after been caught smuggling by Joseph Carter a sitter of the prevention customs belonging to Swanage. Joseph whilst on duty at Haven House near Studland noticed a suspicious light. Hiding under seaweed on the shore saw two men John Galton and Timothy Ellis a third ran away. The two were placing tubs into a boat on the quay. The two were taken away placed in custody and lodged at the watch house. Later the two were taken, impressed into the navy, and transferred to an Algerine sloop.

Officers of the impress service would at all times hold a large supply of warrants and also at their disposal would be a guard ship; one such ship was the *Royal William.* Impressed men would be held on board ready to be moved on.

It was also stressed to the commanders of all the revenue cutters the importance of capturing and securing smugglers for impressments into the navy. To assist with this instruction a financial reward was offered to the top three revenue cutters that secured and delivered over to His Majesty's Naval Service the highest number of smugglers. The highest would receive £500, the second £300 and the third £200 and that would be on top of the £20 per head for each smuggler impressed into the navy. This became known as 'blood money' among the smugglers, adding to hatred of all revenue men.

Smugglers were also given a way of getting a pardon; this was through a committee headed by Sir John Cope who produced a report that resulted with the act of parliament in 1736 known as the 'smugglers act' – act of indemnity, those admitting to smuggling activities before 27 April 1736 would be pardoned, but if caught and found guilty of smuggling after that date, all crimes of smuggling would be considered. The penalty for smuggling if caught after 24 June 1736 could have been transportation to the American plantations for a period of seven years. Offenders were encouraged to snitch on or implicate their fellow smugglers. They would then be let off from the sentence and be paid a reward of maybe £50.

For those caught trying to bribe an official there was a fine of £50. The act of 1736 did have little effect although some smugglers did take advantage of this. A report in the Poole Letter Book of 11 July 1736 shows a report giving information of goods at little Canford, but the report shows that a Thomas changed his mind about the reward of 35 guineas offered and refused it as it was not enough.

A good example of what would become of the smugglers, if caught, was the incident that took place at Christchurch in 1784 and became known as the Battle of Mudeford. The battle raged from 6 p.m. to 9 p.m. and many men were either killed or seriously wounded. It all started with a very large run of tea and spirits (5,000 casks of spirits and 400 chests of tea) from the Channel Islands and brought ashore on 15 July 1784 at Mudeford beach, near the Haven where the car park is today. In 1784 it looked totally different; it would have been a gravel and ironstone beach, a good place to land and run a large cargo of contraband. Awaiting the smugglers was a gang of some 300 willing people ready to unload the cargo from the two luggers *Civil Usage* and the *Phoenix* owned and run by John Streeter on to about 100 carts, drawn by about 400 horses.

During the unloading of the cargo the captain of the naval cutter HMS *Resolution* discovered the events of that night. Realising *Resolution* was heavily outnumbered and out-gunned he sat back and watched the events unfold in front of her. In the meantime, Captain Sarmon lowered the long boat and went in search of assistance, finding it in HMS *Orestes* off the needles and HMS *Swan* in Poole Bay. Then accompanied by two other revenue vessels they rounded Hengistbury Head causing instant panic.

The two vessels unloaded had been moved into Christchurch Harbour ready to be ballasted. One of the most notorious smugglers of Christchurch, John Streeter, who appeared to have crewed on one of the two luggers, was at the time apparently in Christchurch. On hearing of the situation on the shore and the position his vessels were in he rode back to the Haven. He gathered his men and muskets en route and they took up their positions on the Haven - within the Haven Inn, the stables and along the beach within the sandbanks. Seeing the position of his two vessels he ordered them to be beached and then set to and stripped the two luggers of all their lines, rigging and equipment leaving nothing behind for the revenue men.

Whilst all this was going on the loaded carts started to move away from the shore and blended into the surrounding countryside, taking with them an estimated 120,000 gallons of spirits and approximately

25 tons of tea. Later that night when the tide came in the two vessels started to float off the beach and then the marines on board the revenue cutters under cover of darkness floated the two vessels off, and towed them back to Cowes.

The captain of the *Orestes* was looking on whilst this was happening and was determined to capture and seize the contraband and the two luggers. He and the two escorting revenue vessels lowered six rowing boats filled with sailors armed to the teeth. As they closed onto the shore and the two beached luggers he called for the sailors on board to surrender only to be met by a volley of musket fire. At this time the master of the *Orestes,* William Allen, was standing up in the rowing boat, only to fall back mortally wounded. The battle then continued with the smugglers at an advantage as they had dug into ditches on the beach and the revenue men were trying to return fire from a rowing boat with no cover, bobbing up and down in the sea. It is said that William Allen was mortally wounded before any shots were fired by the revenue men.

The battle continued for some hours, with the smugglers retreating to the Haven House and the revenue men dug in on the beach and pinned down, suffering casualties (William Allen eventually died of his injuries at 6 a.m. the next day). The naval lugger even started firing cannon balls and one ball apparently hit the Christchurch Priory about 2 miles away. As darkness fell it became difficult to see who was firing at whom. The smugglers then retreated back to Christchurch; they knew that as a man had died there would be every effort made to track down the culprits who fired the musket that killed William Allen. At the inquest a verdict of wilful murder was reached by the jury. Allen was buried in Cowes with full military honours, the whole ship's crew attending.

From the report by William Arnold no arrest had been made at the time and a reward of £200 was offered to any person who would come forward with information citing two or more persons involved, this was also extended to any smuggler who could identify the person who fired the shot that killed William Allen. A list was then drawn up of suspects and also an estimate of the quantity of goods that was landed on the Haven that evening. The estimate at the time was 120,000 gallons of spirits and about 25 tons of tea. It was also reported that the men concerned should pay treble the value of the goods and John Streeter is mentioned for the treble the value of 42,000 gallons of brandy, rum and gin.

In all there were twenty-seven warrants out for the arrest of smugglers, eight for more serious and capital charges. Eventually three men were caught; as William Allen died on the tide line the three men would be tried under the jurisdiction of the high court of the Admiralty in London. They stood before the bar at the Old Bailey on Tuesday 21 June 1785; two of the men Henry Voss and Jonathan Edwards were released and the third George Coombes was found guilty of the murder of William Allen and taken to Execution Dock where he was hanged. His body was then hung in chains at Haven House point, until cut down by sympathizers and given a decent burial.

If you were unlucky enough to be caught the penalty was not always as harsh as this; sometimes it was quite lenient as is shown within the reports and articles within the *Salisbury and Winchester Journal.* In many cases the magistrates would have benefited from the smugglers activities and in some cases they may even have been involved, putting up the money to purchase the vessels and organizing the cargoes, whereas the average smuggler would have been fishermen or farm labours looking to supplement their meagre wages and to be able to support their family. The wealthy landowners and gentry have also been known to pay the fines imposed by the courts, thus sparing the smugglers a term in the local gaol.

There is also evidence of the gentry and landowners turning a blind eye claiming they have seen nothing as is shown here: Edward Hooper was entertaining Lord Shaftesbury (chairman of the Customs and Excise) at Heron Court now known as Hurn Court near Christchurch. The house was on one of the major routes used by the smugglers to bring contraband inland. Whilst at dinner there was the sound of six or seven wagons heavily loaded with tubs rushing past the window at full gallop. Lord Shaftesbury jumped to his feet looking at the spectacle as it rolled past, but Edward Hooper stayed in his seat with his back to the window and completed his meal. Soon afterward a troop of dragoons followed on horseback, stopped and asked if they had seen anything and which way the smugglers had gone. To which Hooper could truthfully say he saw nothing and nobody could say for sure which way the smugglers had gone.

Revd Richard Warner recounts in his Literary Recollections of an incident that occurred in the early part of the nineteenth century when he witnessed a procession of between twenty and thirty wagons loaded with kegs of spirits and an armed man sitting at the front and rear and surrounded by a large troop of about two or three hundred horsemen, all carrying on their saddles two to four tubs of spirits winding their way along the skirts of Hengistbury Head, heading north-west of Christchurch.

Large rewards were offered for any information relating to the cases of severe brutality meted out against the revenue men, but it was not wise to give them information about your fellow smugglers. The smuggler's reprisals could be just as savage, if not more brutal, than the revenue men. Smugglers looked on the revenue men and the informers as the enemy and treated them as such. An incident occurred reported on 20 December 1762 in the *Salisbury and Winchester Journal* when a gang of smugglers broke into the house of William Manuel at Iford and dragged his son Joseph out of the house towards Poole across the heath to a lone house called Decoy Pond House, a place frequented by many smugglers. From there he was placed on a boat and then forcibly taken by a smuggling vessel to Alderney. He managed to escape but only after being severely injured. This was all because his father had supposedly given information to the revenue officers. A reward was posted of £50 for any information to bring the culprits to justice.

To show the size of rewards offered, in November 1827 a reward of £200 was offered and a gracious pardon for persons who were present or aiding in such an outrageous act and to pass on any information on the incident that occurred on the eve of Wednesday, 19 September when at Swanage within the Port of Poole in the county of Dorset a gang of about seventy smugglers armed with fire arms, swords and swingles attacked the chief officer and the crew of the revenue cutter. The pardon and reward offered did not actually apply to those who carried out the act and assaulted the officers.

Showing how dangerous the profession of being a revenue man was could be seen in the incident of the night of 24 August 1780. John Bursey was a good officer and was tireless in his attack on the smuggling within the surrounding area. That night two men knocked on his door claiming to take him to the site of hidden contraband and wishing to claim the reward. As he stepped outside the two men attacked him and severely beat him around the head whilst his family looked on. His wife tried to help her husband but was met with blunderbuss being fired at her, followed by threats on her life along with her children. His injuries were so severe that he died from them three days later. This was not an uncommon incident.

But for a spy there was a special punishment awaiting: being pinned out on the beach at low tide and then waiting for the tide to come in. The lucky ones may just have got away with a flogging.

But on the other hand if you helped the smugglers as did a Dr Quartley of Christchurch you would be rewarded. One evening he was taken from his house to remove a slug from the shoulder of a wounded smuggler. The next day he found a tub of brandy on his door step. Strangely, many years later, the fellow made himself known to the doctor as he rowed the doctor on the River Avon.

If an officer was injured whilst on duty in 1780, custom commissioners paid a disability pension to the injured officers. This was paid at £10 per annum to those that lost a hand, foot or greater injury and also all surgeons bills would be paid, and from 1820 the revenue men were granted a pension.

There are many stories of smugglers escaping the grasp of the revenue men and here is but one. An old fellow of the name George King lived at Longham and died a self-confessed smuggler in 1875. He was introduced to the trade in 1820 and remembered a landing that occurred at Bournemouth where there were 550 men waiting on the beach, but also present on the beach was 'preventer' men. They came down the hill and as they did so King grasped two of the kegs and slung them over his shoulder. 'This great feller' then slashed at King's shoulder who instantly dropped the two kegs and they fell to the ground. He then turned and gripped one of the kegs. On that night only nine kegs were saved, the remaining cargo was seized and taken to the custom house.

But at the same time there are examples of the revenue officers not wanting to get involved but in fact letting the smugglers ply their trade unhindered. For example, in 1777 whilst a group of smugglers ran a cargo ashore and landed 20 tons of tea brought over from Dunkirk, the customs men just sat and watched the events unfold in front of them, mainly because just off shore was the armed smugglers vessel carrying 24-pounders aimed at the beach. The tea was loaded onto three carriages and taken inland, but they left 12 cwt. of tea on the beach, which the customs officials went down and seized only to have it liberated by 30–40 smugglers who returned to the beach to collect it. The custom men were severely beaten and cut for their troubles.

As for intimidation of the revenue officers, this also did occur as referred to in a letter dated 1804 in the Poole Letter Book which hinted towards intimidation against the officers and that they may have been under the influence of the smugglers, and prevented from carrying out their duty purely by fear of what might become of them if they did so. This is supported by an incident a few years earlier, in 1799, when a Parkstone riding officer was attacked by three smugglers and before that a riding officer from Milford had his saddle girth cut.

Age was not taken into consideration when the custom officers would take on the smugglers as the incident on Weymouth coast in December 1832 showed when a boy of fifteen years of age was killed whilst landing a cargo and been intercepted by Revenue Cutter *Eagle*. The story goes that the boy was shot by the coastguard while assisting his master in carrying away tubs from the beach that had been landed. It was reported in the *Salisbury and Winchester Journal* of 31 December 1832. Another tells of a serious affray that took place on Weymouth coast on Sunday morning at about 2 a.m. between the smugglers and the preventative men who were stationed at Weymouth. In all approximately 100 smugglers were found to be working the contraband on the beach opposite Lodmoor. Having run most of the contraband they were discovered by the two preventative men who seized the remaining contraband. The smugglers, not wanting to lose the contraband, tried to recover the goods coming into contact with the preventative men who had arrived on the spot along with a crew from the cutter *Eagle*. The cutter started firing powder, not wanting to hurt the crew and preventative men but to try and protect the seized kegs. The cutter then started firing balls; the result was a large amount of blood left on the beach, many injuries and two deaths - a smuggler called 'Brown' aged twenty and John Webber aged fifteen. Many of the smugglers were injured and one of the preventative men was also injured quite severely. In all sixty-six casks were seized. Which along with the bodies were probably taken to Weymouth. John Webber was buried in the parish of Sydling St Nicholas on 30 December 1832.

At the height of smuggling it was estimated that as many as 25,000 men were employed or in some way involved in smuggling activities along the South Coast and to show the dedication to the trade within an hour's notice gangs of up to 500 men could be assembled at any spot to help unload and take the illicit cargoes away. Some would be heavily armed ready to protect the valuable cargo at any cost, including loss of life.

To show the level of smuggling figures for the illicit import of tea, 4 million lb of tea was brought into the country and from that 3.2 million lb was brought into the country through smuggling, with an incredible loss of duty to the country. The tea mainly came into the country via Holland as they were not great tea drinkers, the surplus tea being sold to traders/smugglers. The wines, spirits and tobacco would have come into the country via Roscoff and Cherbourg in France and also via the Channel Islands.

Spirits would normally be in a 4 gallon tubs and the tea would be packed in waterproof sacks and then loaded into the casks. The bulk of the contraband brought into Dorset was brandy and wine as can be seen by the lists of seizures in the custom Letter Books. Other commodities such as tea, coffee, tobacco silks, raisins, figs and perfumes were also imported as can be seen by the lists of commodities advertised for auction in the *Salisbury and Winchester Journal.*

Lists of seizures at Weymouth in 1824

In the month of January, they seized 251 casks of foreign spirits and again in Feb of 1824 they seized 114 casks of foreign spirits, along with a man called Joseph Rush who was taken by William Hambly and convicted and fined £100. He defaulted on the fine and was committed to Dorchester gaol. Again in January 1826, 149 casks of foreign spirits were seized and deposited in the customs warehouse.

List of seized commodities was advertised for auction in the *Salisbury and Winchester Journal* on 22 January 1781:

> On the 25 January at 2 p.m. in the afternoon will be exposed to public sale at the custom house of this port (Poole):
>
> Brandy 133 gallons
>
> Rum 278 gallons

Geneva 1559 gallons

Claret 120 gallons

Rhubarb 6½lb

Denia Raisons 2cwt. 2qrs 14lb

Currants 2cwt. 0qrs 25lb

Pitch 13cwt. 0qrs 13lb

Nankeen 160 pieces

Raw Coffee 158lb

Tea Bohea 9,237lb

Hyfon 202lb

Souchong 310lb

Green 242lb

Also offered at this particular sale were a cart and a boat along with a parcel of tobacco ash. 27 August 1781. On the 30 August at 2 p.m. in the afternoon will be exposed to public sale at the custom house of this port (Poole):

Brandy 111 gallons

Rum 10 gallons

Geneva 671 gallons

1 packet of Tobacco ashes

And finally to show the extents of seizures on the 28 April 1829 by the order of the Honourable Commissioners of his Majesty at 11 a.m. in the forenoon will be exposed to public sale at the Custom House Weymouth (at a price not less than the duty):

1,300 Gallons of Brandy

250 Gallons of Geneva (Gin)

1 Silver Waist Band

2 Pair Bracelets

2 Silk Handkerchiefs

18 Staves, above 36 and not exceeding 50in in Length

5 Pieces – Quantity 79 Feet Fir Timber

11 Pair Kid Gloves

2 Pairs Silk Stockings.

2 Linen Sheets

7lb Verdigris

3 Pieces of Rope

8 Glass Tumblers

3 Fancy Boxes

Also for sale was the sloop *Juliana* measuring 13 feet, 48–94 tons with all her tackle, apparel and furniture, and materials of destroyed 4-gallon casks.

The goods would then be available for viewing by applying to the custom house two days prior to the sale.

If a vessel was captured, the cargo and the vessel itself would be seized and a report sent to the exchequer who would instruct the Mayor of the port where the vessel was taken to hold a special court, the goods and vessel would be valued and offered for public sale and sold to the highest bidder, as seen above. When the auction was over, the proceeds would go to the exchequer and 1/3rd of the proceeds would go to the crew and officers to be divided up among them and divided as shown below:

The Commander 14/32nds

The Mate 7/32nds

Deputed Mariner 3/32nds exclusive of his share as Mariner

Other Mariners 8/32nds

No wonder with the prospect of large sums of money to be earned that the revenue cutters would be anxious to earn their share of the pickings.

If the hull of a vessel touched the bottom, then the vessel became the property of the crown subject to local variations. Any items that floated off a vessel at sea, and which was picked up at sea is known as flotsam; goods jettisoned, for example, to lighten a vessel is jetsam and are both the responsibility of the admiralty.

If the smugglers were lucky, and managed to evade the revenue men when disposing of their contraband, the smugglers would price their cargo accordingly to landing place; for example a 4 gallon cask of brandy would cost the smugglers in Cherbourg about 7*s* 6*d* and the price of freight for a cask would be about 8s and if sold at sea would cost ½ guinea or 11*s*, if landed between Hurst Castle and Christchurch, under the protection of guns, and put into possession of land smugglers a further 6*s* per tub would be charged; if brought within the Isle of Wight or Langston/Portsmouth price would go up to 1 guinea per cask, (21*s*) making a tidy profit for the smugglers.

It is also said that as long as the smugglers landed and ran one in three of their cargoes then they would still be in profit. Between 1825 and 1840 a tub of brandy in France would cost 16*s* to 18*s* and about £1 in expenses. Duty at the time on a gallon of spirits was about 36*s*. The suppliers in France would also give twenty-one tubs to the score and also for every 100 tubs supplied they would add two more to cover 'scorage' which would be damage and losses in transit. Another trick they used would be to import high proof spirits to which they would add water. This would increase the quantity of spirit they had available. To ensure the spirits were the correct colour they would add burnt sugar.

Failure of the revenue men is shown in a letter from Capt. F. Marryats. He states that not one tub in ten falls into the hands of those employed against the smugglers.

The value of the cargo is indicated by a receipt for casks of brandy, rum and other items that was found in the wall of the George Inn at Weymouth in 1885. The receipt is as shown below:

Mr Mathew Voss, but of Peter Le Coq April 24th 1776

5 casks Brandy @ 16/6 £6-12-0

7 casks Rum @ 15/6 £5-12-6

One Dozen?

1 Flagon Rum @ £0-11-0

1 cask to put Scorage @ £0-1-6

24Ibs B.Tea in papers @ £1-12-0

£14-5-0

17 September 1776 of Mathew Voss the sum of fourteen pounds five shillings for Mr P Le Coq

Theo Martin

14 March 1776 Received of Mr Mathew Voss the sum of £13 in part payment of amount

£13.0.0 – Peter Le Coq

Dorchester Gaol

After being condemned, Dorchester Gaol was replaced in 1787 but after only a short period of time this prison was also condemned, only to be replaced again in 1795 on a plan approved by Mr Howard in 1788 at a cost of £16,179 10*s* 6*d.*

In 1795 the prison, which still stands today, opened its doors. It was a far cry from the old prison, but still not a place you wanted to end up in. The new prison was built with cell blocks like the spokes of a wheel radiating out from a central octagon. With eighty-eight sleeping cells, besides all the cells for the condemned prisoners, all classes of prisoners would be separated; there is evidence of this as when you read the inspection reports by the clerk of the peace in 1844. There is mention of the smugglers' wing; there was also a store room, an infirmary with two large dormitories for male debtors. In addition to the cells in the debtors' wing there were two large dormitories for the female debtors and female fines, along with a dark room for the refectory. Also included was a bath house, workshops, water closets and a brew house. The new prison was built on the site of the old medieval castle and all public executions took place outside the main gates on the site of the present prison car park in North Square. The last public hanging took place on 10 August 1858 with the execution of James Seal and the last private execution took place in 1941 with the execution of David Jennings aged twenty-one.

The prisoners were well looked after with good food of bread, meat and broth with special diets/ meals for young children and the sick. A special meal at Whitson and Christmas was also provided. The prisoners would sleep on an iron framed bed and a mattress, which more than likely was a canvas bag stuffed with straw.

Those prisoners sentenced to hard labour would leave the prison and would go off to work in a smock with the words Dorchester Gaol written on it. These prisoners would receive an income of which ⅔ would go towards the running of the prison, $^1/_6$ going to the gaoler to encourage him to be attentive or as a gratuity for his trouble, and $^1/_6$ would go to the prisoner, ½ of which would be kept and passed to him when he or she was released and the remainder he or she would use to purchase any indulgence allowed in accordance with the prison rules. That part held by the prison and to be passed to the prisoners when they had completed their sentence could be at any time forfeited if the prisoner misbehaved; no wonder there was little trouble in the prison! The behaviour column within the prison records shows that the majority did behave in an orderly fashion although there are records of those that did misbehave, for example - Job Stokes, John Leg and William Jacobs, all smugglers, are shown to have been disorderly and troublesome whilst in Dorchester Gaol.

The prison inspection reports show what it must have been like and how religion played a large part in prison life and that the prisoners did listen to the prison Chaplin. They also indicate that the Chaplin had difficulty in introducing religion to the smugglers and getting them to reflect back on their crimes and to understand what they had done was wrong. The 1844 inspection by the Clerk of the peace reports on how orderly the prisoners were, mentions their good health and how well the prisoners were looked after. However, he does mention in the report of some disorderly conduct within the smugglers' ward and this is shown in the prison records. Also mentioned was the success of the school at the prison run by a Mr Carter and that there were seventy-two prisoners of different classes and of whom thirty-one were discharged and of these fourteen were able to read and write before they left, four were tolerable whilst the thirteen remaining were not ignorant of their letters but could read imperfectly.

Dorchester Gaol – Punishments Imposed

The records at Dorchester Gaol are quite comprehensive, listing everything about the inmate including any distinguishing marks and the colour of their eyes, but the most interesting part for me was what they had done to be put in jail, and even stranger the age of the inmates. Three youths, the youngest only thirteen, were all sentenced to six months for smuggling. These were William Driver in 1825, Charles Bishop in 1835 and Edward Atwell in 1835.

At the other extreme the oldest was Robert Barrett, a labourer, aged eighty-one who was sent to Dorchester Gaol in 1826 and sentenced to a fine of £50 or four months. Reading through the records I came across many entries for women and even young girls. The youngest girl I found was a Rebecca Sweet from Portland aged fourteen and imprisoned in 1833 for smuggling with a fine of £5 or three weeks. The oldest women I found was a Catherine Winter, a tailor; infact I found two entries for her, one in 1842 at the age of seventy imprisoned for six months but released after only serving eighteen days and again two years later in 1844 at the ripe old age of seventy-three. She was once again imprisoned for one month, both times for smuggling.

I came across seventy-one entries for women imprisoned in Dorchester and the records show that some of them brought their babies into the prison with them. In one case Susannah Stone actually lost her child; the infant died and was taken away on 11 June 1829. Women were also sentenced to hard labour. In 1822 Martha Lumb of Weymouth was sentenced to three months' hard labour for smuggling.

Comparing the lists of offences and the sentenced imposed, those caught smuggling normally end up with just a fine ranging from £5 to £100. If you were unable to pay the fine you would then spend some time at His Majesty's pleasure until the fine was paid or you were released; this could be one month or as some entries show fourteen months. If it was more than just smuggling you could end up with a sentence of hard labour, and if you assaulted or injured a revenue officer in the course of his duties or 'unlawfully assembling armed for illegal purpose' the sentence was death, although I have not found any entry where this sentence was carried out. In each case they were reprieved and sentenced to hard labour over a number of years.

Then there was William Whittle at the age of twenty-three in 1834, whilst smuggling and assaulting a revenue officer was sentenced at Dorchester Assizes to death but once again reprieved and sentenced to ten years' transportation and was put on board the York Hull in Gosport Harbour. There are many entries where the prisoners have been put on board HMS *Queen Charlotte* ready to be impressed into the navy as happened to James Taylor in 1823 aged twenty-seven and James Harris in 1819 aged thirty-nine.

Others received lesser sentences; for example, John Byatt in 1827 aged sixty-three was signalling a vessel at sea or as the entry shows 'making a light on sea coast to assist the smugglers'. For this crime at the age of sixty-three he was sentenced to six months' hard labour. It is also true that the smugglers were punished much more harshly than other criminals, although the sentences were a lot less harsh in comparison. For example, a petty criminal could end up been transported for stealing a loaf of bread, and if you carried out a burglary you may end up at the gallows.

The prisoners came from all walks of life and professions, mainly professions that worked outside in the open. Fishermen, labourers, ships pilots, quarrymen and flax growers all feature in the records but there were a few that worked in doors such as butchers and servants. So to be confined in a small cell and locked away must have driven some of them mad and been very difficult for them. Surprisingly the inmates seem to come from all over the country not just Dorset although the majority of them did come from Dorset. Neighbouring counties feature quite often but some prisoners came from as far away as Kent, Sussex, London, Bristol, Berkshire, Glamorganshire, Pembrokeshire, Shropshire, and Staffordshire. So in some cases they were a long way from home, which must have placed a strain on them and their families. There were even prisoners from France, Ireland and The Channel Islands.

6

Smuggling Vessels and the Acts that tried to stop them

Reading the Letter Books from Cowes, Poole and Weymouth, things must have got pretty bad, for in the Weymouth Letter Book the entry dated 11 December 1718 is a directive from the commissioners which states that:

For prevention of any loss of damage by fire to ships or merchandise by officers searching for prohibited goods the commissioners direct: That no Tidesman do presume to search or rummage in the hold or between decks without the presence of the surveyor unless the Tidesman has particular information. That no officers do at any time go into the hold or between decks to search, with candle unless the same is well secured in a lanthorne, on pain of dismissal.

I have used many reports from local papers of the time, such as the *Salisbury and Winchester Journal* and the *Dorset Herald*. Some reports detail some harrowing stories: the *Salisbury and Winchester Journal* reported that on the night of 4 August 1784 there was a skirmish between the crews of some revenue vessels and a gang of smugglers on the North Shore near this port (Poole) one of the gang and his horse were killed. The report does not state who was involved, but it examined the state of the smuggling within the area stating it was of an alarming height to such an extent that a night scarcely went by without a skirmish, which too frequently endeds up with a fatality to one of the parties involved.

The reports become increasingly harrowing and using the reports from the newspapers and from the customs men this book tries to show how difficult it must have been to beat the revenue vessels and also to show how devious the smugglers could be in hiding the contraband and eluding the revenue vessels.

Another success for the revenue men came in July 1824 when Lt Umfreville of the coastguard station at Poole, caught the *Phaedra* yacht of London with sixty-six packages of tobacco weighing between 6–7 cwt., and 6lb of tea. The vessel and three crew members were brought into the Port of Poole and the cargo seized and placed into her majesty's warehouse, and the three crew members secured in gaol.

But accidents and loss of life do occur as shown in the Weymouth Letter Book when an entire section of revenue officers were drowned when the King's boat sank on 25 April 1770 whilst looking out for smugglers: John Bishop, tide surveyor; a number of established boatmen and tidesmen: John Hickman; Thomas Andrew; John Pearce; and Robert Johnson. Also, Thomas Bagg an extra tidesmen; and boatman and coal meter. It is reported that part of the boat came ashore about 9 a.m. on 26 April, 3 miles from Weymouth, and nearby John Hickman came ashore whereupon he was buried. A petition for the widow's families was raised and transmitted.

The revenue then asked for a new boat and materials to replace the lost vessel, meanwhile they borrowed a boat off Captain Lisle until the replacement arrived. The next entry of 4 July 1770 acknowledged the receipt of the replacement vessel from London but unfortunately the vessel was not suitable. In fact, they describe it as 'unfit in every respect out of proper dimensions nor planed for going through the water in so swift a manner as the nature of the service do require'. They then acquaint the authorities for the great necessity for as good a boat as can be planned to row with six oars or else his Majesty's revenue may greatly suffer.

There were many custom/revenue cutters in the service, and they had a colourful and interesting career, a few of which I have listed below with some interesting success stories.

Adelaide – based in Weymouth – weighing in at 143 tons – crew thirty; commanded by C.C W.H. Miller (22 January 1815)

Alarm – Based in Poole

Anson – There was a report in the *Salisbury and Winchester Journal* on 28 January 1747 – Saturday last a seizure of 164 casks of liquors and about 1.5 ton of tea which was brought to his Majesty's warehouse by the crew of the Anson cutter.

In 1767 at Boscombe Chine the crew of the cutter *Anson* attempted to seize 3 tons of tea. The boat crew of five from the *Anson* were attacked on shore by a gang of fifty smugglers, who seized three of the crew, beat them up and threw them into the sea and captured the other two.

Another report within the *Salisbury and Winchester Journal* dated 7 January 1774 tells of a seizure made on board the Anson cutter may be dependent on as fact:

> The 21st of October last Mr Prigg supervisor of excise, and two inferior officers went on board the said cutter, lying then at Brownsea, to search for materials for making candles, and in the search found three six gallon casks of spirits in the foremasts-man's apartment. On that the officers coming ashore Leut Walfon (commander of the cutter) and ordered all hands up on deck, and examined them about the said casks, but all denied they knew anything of them, for fear of punishment according to the rules of the service. Leut Walfon then ordered seizure to be made of them, which accordingly done by a

deputation officers belonging to the cutter, who secured them in the cabin till opportunity presented to send them to the King's warehouse.

Asp – Based at Lyme – weighing in at 45 tons – crew of ten and commanded by C.S.M Henry Harvey (17 June 1843) and Jospeh T. Nash (4 June 1847).

Batt – cutter – Commander Mr James Williams.

Beehive – Cutter Belonging to Warren Lisle Esq. Commanded by Mr James Willis – 1738 (an ex smuggling vessel seized and sold at a public auction)

Report in the Weymouth Letter Book dated 4 September 1738 tells of an incident involving the *Beehive* and the *Diamond* a tender belonging to the *Lenox, a* man-o'-war. The day before they saw a small vessel stand in for the land off Portland, and as soon as they made the *Beehive* they immediately changed course and stood close by the wind, the *Beehive* did the same, and after a chase lasting five hours came up upon the smugglers vessel, but as the smugglers vessel had more hands than the *Beehive* it refused to bring to, upon which Mr Johnson (chief mate) made a signal to the *Diamond* a tender belonging to the *Lenox* man-o'-war to come to their assistance which they did, and Lt Hough Forbes of the Lenox and Mr Johnson boarded the said smuggling vessel bringing it into port whilst towing the tender. The tender broke loose which meant that the tender from the *Beehive* had to be hoisted and put out with one of Mr Johnson's men. John Hastings master of the smuggling vessel saw an opportunity to escape, finding a means to get Lt Hough Forbes, Johnson and the remaining crew members into the great cabin. He then shut them in and nailed them up. The tender was then hoisted up and the smugglers put to the wind sailing off with Lt Hough Forbes, Johnson and two of his men on board. There is a later report in the Weymouth Letter Book dated 20 September 1738 which shows that Lt Hough Forbes, Johnson and his two men were taken to Boulogne in France and landed.

A good example of 'hovering' and been caught was when in October 1764 a report in the *Salisbury and Winchester Journal* tells of how on 3 October 1764, the *Bee- Hive* in the service of the customs brought into and deposited in the custom house thirty hundred weight of tea which was seized out of a smuggling cutter hovering on the coast.

Cholmondeley – sloop – Captain Warren Lisle – 1741.

Diligence – based in Weymouth. On 27 September 1783 seized and brought into port a large quantity of foreign spirituous liquor which was secured in her Majesty's warehouse.

On 4 December 1783 seized and brought into port a large quantity of foreign spirituous liquor and tea which was secured in her Majesty's warehouse.

Eagle – based in Weymouth – weighing in at 100 tons – with a crew of twenty-three – commanded by Lt St Quinton (March 1829) and Lt Commander John Allen (16 June 1845). On 6 March 1829 the *Eagle* detained the sloop, *Eliza*; the cargo appears to have been destroyed.

On 6 March 1829 the *Eagle* chased and detained the sloop *La Concorde*, from Cherbourg, off Portland. On board were a crew of seven: four French and three English. The penalties for smuggling could be severe and so to avoid this, the smugglers would try and destroy the evidence, in this case throwing the cargo overboard. Ten casks were picked up and deposited in the Weymouth Customs House. Their cargoes were not always just spirits and tea. On this occasion, one of the casks was packed very carefully with 1,000 yards of silk.

The *Eagle* took part in the Battle on Weymouth Beach in 1832 when a fifteen-year-old boy, John Webber, lost his life.

Fancy – Revenue cutter. Report within the Dorset County Chronicles and Somersetshire Gazette tell of the revenue cutter *Fancy* commanded by Lt Spark RN capturing and bringing into the Port of Poole the smuggling vessel 'Intergrity' along with her crew and a cargo of 157 casks of brandy and gin. She was captured at around 1 a.m. on 9 February 1829 by a boat rowing guard off Studland. The vessels must have been lying off the coast for some days as signals and fires had been observed from the Purbeck hills for several nights.

Fox – revenue cutter – weighing in at 34 tons. The revenue cutter under the command of Lt Scale arrived in the Port of Weymouth April 1826 with 106 tubs of spirits the remaining part of the cargo from the French smuggling vessel *Pharbe*. She was chased on the night of the 7th when she was obliged to cut away her boat and destroy the greater part of her cargo.

Gertrude – Based in Swanage – Weighing in at 35 tons – crew of eight – commanded by D.O John Super (9 August 1841).

Garland – Based in Poole. Saw active service against the French when William Weston collector at Weymouth was wounded along with one seaman on 15 August 1801 during an attack on Boulogne under the command of Lord Nelson.

Greyhound I – Weighing in at 200 tons, with a crew of forty-five men, Stationed in Weymouth 1793–1805 with a letter of Marque. Cutter armed with sixteen guns: both 9- and 6-pounders, commanders Stephen Watson and Captain Richard Wilkinson. Vessels captured:

Surprise – 51 tons – May 1793

Hero – 15 tons – June 1797

Jarratt – 38 tons – November 1801

Go – 43 tons – August 1805

Captain Wilkinson whilst in command seems to have had a very active career capturing many French privateers: the *Actiffe* in 1793, the *Custine* in 1793 and on 21st March 1797 captured the French privateer *Liberté* near Cape Barfleur just to name a few. It appears also he fought the French on 15 August 1801 at Boulogne under Lord Nelson where he, along with one of his seamen, was injured.

Greyhound II – Stationed at Weymouth 1813–1821 with letter of Marque. Cutter 1st class, English customs. Built in 1808 by William Good of Bridport. Weighing in at 150 tons and armed with twelve 9-pounders. Captain and owner Richard Wilkinson. It seemed to have a distinguished life as it was also stationed at Grimsby in 1839 and Leith in 1844 only to be paid off on 24 May 1849.

Hawke – Whilst cruising off West Lulworth in October 1818 commanded by Lt Ward, seized fifty kegs of foreign spirits which was lodged at the custom house at Poole. Lieutenant Ward also captured the four smugglers off Portland and delivered them to the magistrates at Poole, but with the assistance of a rope they scaled the walls of the prison and made good their escape.

Later in October 1818, whilst laying at Brownsea, a party from the *Hawke* revenue cutter seized seventy-nine kegs of spirits on the North Shore. The vessel, believed to come from either Portland or Weymouth, got into trouble and was forced onto the shore due to bad weather. Luckily no lives were lost but the vessel was swamped and John Davis, one of the crew, was taken into custody.

HMS *Orestes* – Naval brig-sloop, painted yellow and with a capacity of about 300 tons. She was fitted with rowing ports for sweeps and armed with eighteen guns, and captained by Captain Ellis. Originally this vessel was a Dutch privateer called the *Mars* but in 1781 it was captured by the Royal Navy and renamed and impressed into the Royal Navy. HMS *Orestes* was stationed in Studland Bay, a convenient place to keep an eye on Poole Bay and Swanage. To assist in the job of stopping, searching and seizing goods. Under the 'smugglers acts' the collector of Cowes Arnold gave Captain Ellis and his officers special warrants called 'deputations'. Not long after the HMS *Orestes* was stationed in Studland, Captain Ellis noticed a large cutter of about 200 tons hovering off the offing, not taking much notice of the vessel Captain Ellis sailed westward as if making for the channel, on reaching Portland Bill he turned back, hiding around Swanage. Captain Ellis had outwitted the smuggler. Not until the smugglers reached the Needles did they realize that HMS *Orestes* was under full sail and in pursuit, the smuggling vessel tacked and tried with all its might to escape but alas they failed to escape, HMS *Orestes* fired a warning shot which the smuggling vessel ignored only to clear and make ready one of their own guns. Realising what had happened and the smuggling vessels defiance Captain Ellis opened fire with her 9-pounders hitting and damaging the smugglers vessel and injuring a number of her crew. Realising they stood no chance the crew disappeared below and the vessel was seized and taken to Cowes. On boarding the vessel, Captain Ellis found twenty 6-pounders all shotted, primed and cast loose. Her general state was ready for battle, but even for a naval vessel like HMS *Orestes* this would have been a tough fight. The strange thing is, and this gave Arnold a problem, for a vessel over 200 tons the hovering act did not apply and thus the vessel could not be forfeited. In the months that followed the condemnation of the vessel and cargo was produced, that being the vessel, 2,000 gallons of spirits and 9 tons of tea. This would earn Arnold a commission of about £150, and considering his wage was £155 a year, it shows that a tidy profit could be made.

It does not always go the way of the revenue men as this incident shows on 8 June 1784 when HMS *Orestes* was out on patrol when they came across a large smuggling vessel laden fully with tea, but before securing the vessel they were attacked by a large cutter with mounted twenty-two guns which came in from the offing and apparently tried to run them down. They attempted to escape by rowing to windward; the other vessel opened fire and hit the boat killing one man and dangerously two others. They carried on firing until their gunshot was spent, where upon they were hailed and informed of the fact they were from the man-o'-war HMS *Orestes* which resulted in yet another attack on the revenue cutters.

HMS *Orestes* took part in the Battle of Mudeford in 1784.

Laurel – Based in Poole – weighing in at 130 tons. A report in the *Salisbury and Winchester Journal* of 17 December 1764 tells of cutter *Laurel* and *Aston* brought into port a lug sail which they managed to apprehend near Guernsey and they even brought four prisoners who beat the officers, as having obstructed the officers in their duty of searching the vessel. The vessel was loaded with a large quantity of tea and spirits. "The Kings cutters were now going to Portsmouth with their prize."

The *Laurel* has had many battles with smugglers where her crew have been injured or worse killed in action. An entry in the Poole Letter Book dated 22 September 1781 mentions once such incident where a John Vile was injured on execution of his duties whilst on board the Laurel with an engagement between the *Rose*, *Speedwell* and the *Laurel* and a large smuggling vessel off the Isle of Wight on 17 April 1781. The report does not mention the outcome of the battle but does mention that the surgeon from Weymouth attended John Vile and that John Vile was disabled from further service and asked for honours bounty.

According to the Poole Letter Book on 15 June 1782, a boat belonging to the *Laurel* cutter was cruising along shore near St Albans and the crew discovered a lugger lying at anchor at Chapmans Poole which was identified as a smuggling vessel, immediately making towards her, but on coming up and attempting to board her. Several muskets were fired at them from the said lugger at which they made signal to the *Laurel* 'to come to their assistance'. The *Laurel* weighed anchor and ran into Swanage Bay. On boarding the cutter, it was found to be deserted and on inspection only two casks containing 5½ gallons of spirits were recovered, not enough to seize, so the vessel was restored to the owners.

On 31 May 1784 the *Salisbury and Winchester Journal* reported upon an incident on: 'Wednesday last the 25 May 1784 when a large lug sail open boat laden with spirits and tea which was taken by the *Laurel* on the Tuesday, but was rescued by the smugglers after as the report states "dangerously wounding Mr Thomas Vye", second mate on the *Laurel*.'

Nancy – Weighing in at 34 tons and an ex -smuggling vessel, seized and condemned in 1794, belonging to the Wernham brothers from Hastings. Due to the speed of this vessel William Arnold (collector at Cowes) used her on a temporary basis from 3 November 1795 and had her re-fitted out as a customs vessel, commanded by Robert Willis a boatman of the Port of Cowes, and the *Nancy* was to be used on a temporary basis until the replacement for the *Swan III* was built in 1796, but once again the replacement vessel *Swan III* was also seized by the French in December 1796, so the trial period for the *Nancy* as a revenue vessel seemed to be a lot longer than originally anticipated and she continued service until the next year 1798. The *Nancy* had a lot of success under the command of Robert Willis as mentioned in the Cowes Letter Book. An entry of 17 August 1796 tells of how the cutter kept a diligent lookout for smugglers and that they seized upwards of 400 casks of spirits and tobacco along with a Lugsail boat.

Life on board the *Nancy* must have been pretty bad as an entry in Cowes Letter Book of 5 September 1797 mentions the fact that the vessel being a seized vessel, condemned and twelve years old had by now become very leaky not only in her bottom but her upper works and decks, which meant the crew could not stay dry and warm, nor could the cutter stay at sea without great hazard. The *Nancy* really needed a refit, and a full set of new sails. Alas they did not think the vessel was worth the expense, and in 1798 an order was given for the vessel's discontinuance, where upon the vessel was laid aside, broken up and the pieces sold.

An interesting fact which about the pay for commanding the *Nancy*.
Robert Willis – The commander's salary was £30 per annum – commenced 10 March 1796.

Luke Lidiard – A mate and eight mariners on 1s per day; a hard life for little reward.

Pierce – Galley – Stationed at Dartmouth but lent to Weymouth port in 1700 to cover the time the Weymouth smack was been altered so to be fit for service. Captain Lander then went into pursuit of the smugglers vessel for a second time with the *Laurels* boat coming up with them on the Wednesday, but not till they had landed their cargo, there once again was a skirmish and it is supposed that one of the smugglers was killed and others wounded on the shore Captain Lander managed to retake the smugglers vessel and bring it into this port (Poole).

Peterel – based in Weymouth – weighing in at 60 tons, crew of sixteen commanded by C.F.M David Lowe (25 January 1843).

Rambler – On 5 July 1784 the *Salisbury and Winchester Journal* reported that his Majesty's cutter *Rambler* fell in with a smuggling lugger belonging to Little Hampton off the Isle of Wight. The chase continued for three hours. Falling calm the crew of the *Rambler* decided to put out its boat with the intention of boarding the lugger, but the smuggling vessel was with cutlasses and a desperate engagement ensued in which two of them were killed and their Captain Wilson was desperately wounded and the remaining crew surrendered. The vessel was then searched and the following contraband was found and seized: 300 tubs of gin and seventy-five bags of tea.

Ranger – in October 1822 in a gale the *Ranger* struck Hasbro Sands. All but seven and one man, who was ashore sick, of her forty crew perished.

Resolution – took part in the Battle of Mudeford in 1784.

Rob Roy – based in Weymouth – weighing in at 52 tons – crew fourteen – commanded by C.S.M Adam Grieve (25 January 1845).

Rose – Based in Southampton – in 1784 the 'Rose' brought into Southampton a smuggling brig with 1,000 kegs of sprits a quantity of Tea and Wine.

Took part in the Battle of Mudeford in 1784

The following appeared in the *London Gazette*:

> Whereas it has been represented to the Commissioners of HM Customs, that on the 10 Dec 1790, as James Cammell, Second Mate of the Rose Revenue Cutter was cruising between Christchurch and Hurst, in a Boat belonging to the said Cutter, he fell in with a large smuggling lugger near Becken Bury, and which was then landing her Cargo: That on his being discovered by the Crew of the said Lugger, they ordered him to come on Board, which the Officer refused, and immediately the

> Lugger got under Sail, chased the Custom-House Boat, and feloniously fired several Shot at her.

Interestingly though, in 1825 the entire crew of the *Rose* was dismissed for seeking to run tobacco.

Scorpion – Sloop commanded in 1759 by Captain Cleland. On 3 July 1759 Captain Cleland seized five bags at 32lb of Bohea tea, two bags at 42lb of raw coffee and thirty-nine casks which was 231½ gallons of brandy, all coming from a small sloop approximately 2 leagues off Peveril Point, and sent it to the collector by Lt Bowers for his care and to take proper steps to get it condemned and sold. The captain's share from the sale was £26 13*s* 10½*d.*

Sherborne – another of Captain Lisle's vessels, based in Lyme Regis.

Spider – Based in Poole.

Speedwell – Based in Weymouth – a sloop – weighing 194 tons, with a crew of thirty-one – Captain in 1755 was James Webb.

Swan I – Wrecked on her maiden voyage, sunk near the needles. The Swan under the command of George Sarmon was at the time looking for the Christchurch smuggler John Streeter when the Swan was lost. The Needles Channel was a dangerous place any time but in a gale it made it even more so, and George Sarmon should have waited for the weather to ease before attempting the channel, but he did not with disastrous results, the loss of the *Swan.* A sudden gust of wind drove them onto the shingle, but the *Swan* itself was battered to pieces by the waves. After the storm had passed George Sarmon and his mate returned to the site to recover the guns and as much of the iron works as they could.

Swan II – Weighing in at 90 tons with a crew of twenty-five and armed with ten 6-pounders. Fought at the battle of Mudeford in 1784 and in 1792 seized 1,000 tubs at Bournemouth, but in the same year was wrecked near Shoreham.

On 29 May 1784 the *Salisbury and Winchester Journal* reported that a boat belonging to the revenue cutter *Swan* of this port (Cowes) fell in with a large tub boat off Christchurch Head laden with tea and spirits making for the shore and attempting to run alongside her was immediately fired upon by the smugglers. It appears that four of the *Swan's* crew were 'dangerously wounded'. Another larger smuggling vessel came to the aid of the tub boat and the *Swan* crew were taken on board the larger armed smuggling cutter. The article then says, 'This is another instance of the desperate pitch to which smuggling has now arrived'.

Swan III – Built in 1793 and captured by two French privateers in October 1795.

Swan IV – Weighing in at 120 tons. In December 1796 she was also captured by the French after a fight with a large French cruiser, in this fight her captain, Captain Sarmon, was killed (by a shot to the forehead from a musket) but the ship was later recaptured from the French by the Royal Navy.

Swan V – Built in 1799 and captured on 19 March 1807 by three large French vessels off The Needles, taking their prize and Captain Richard Combes (who was the mate to Captain Sarmon) back to France, only to return seven years later to face disgrace and dismissal.

Swift –

Tartar – Commanded by Lt Porter. In February 1833 the revenue cruiser, under the command of Lt Porter, chased and captured a smuggling vessel carrying 160 tubs of spirits, which was taken and secured at the Custom House in Poole. The crew of seven: consisting of four English men and three French men were taken and lodged in gaol.

Vulcan – based in Weymouth – weighing at 325 tons – H.P 150 – 37 crew commanded by Lt Commander C.H Baker (29 January 1844) and Lt Commander J.A Pritchard (1-01-1848)

Walker – sloop – Captain Warren Lisle – in 1734 Captain Lisle took over the vessel and found the vessel to be in such a sorry state he bought the vessel off the crown and completely refitted her. He then hired her back to the Collector of Weymouth at a rate of two shillings and sixpence per month per ton.

Lisle had many success stories but in 1737 he seized a cutter, Guernsey Packet. which had been used for smuggling on the Channel Island route. On receipt of his share of the seizure he paid it to the crown and refitted the vessel and re-named it the *Beehive.*

Weymouth – smack – Captain Winslow 1699–1703 – wrecked. In the Weymouth Letter Book there is an entry dated 24 April 1700 where they were considering the unfitness of the smack and the requirement to lengthen her to make her more useful to the station at an estimated cost of £7. They were then directed to get the vessel lengthened but not to leave the coast unguarded in the meantime. Captain Winslow was told to go to Dartmouth to take possession of the galley *Pierce* to be used to cover the coastal area until the Weymouth smack was ready and fit for service.

Later on in the Weymouth Letter Book there is an entry to do with the loss of the *Weymouth* stating that Captain Winslow cannot be held totally responsible for the loss of the vessel at a time of war (with France). It also appears that due to the war with France a replacement vessel was not forth coming and it was recommended that in the meantime the officers within the surrounding limits of the Port of Weymouth to be quickened on this occasion and to be more diligent in their respective stations.

Other revenue cutters operating in the area: the *Queenbro* – smack – 1733 stationed in Rochester; *King George II* – 1733 stationed at Gravesend; *Duke of Cornwall* – sloop 1738 – operated along the Dorset Coast; *Princess Royal* – sloop – 1748 – stationed at Dartmouth; *Amelia* – sloop – Nathan Pigram – 1752 – stationed at Rye; *Richmond* – cutter – Captain Pierce – 1761 – stationed at Chichester; *Ranger* – Cutter – Captain Fraser – 1808 – stationed at Plymouth; *Busy* – cutter – 1808 – stationed at Plymouth.

An additional fact I came across is that any vessel in the Royal Navy with less than twenty-nine guns was known as a sloop and had a compliment of six officers, sixteen mariners and seventy-two seamen.

Boat Builders

William Arnold was collector at Cowes from 1777 to 1800; he also built vessels to wage war on the smugglers in order to stem the illicit trade. Another important builder was Richard Pinney of Poole, later known as Pinney Adams.

The Poole Letter Book's entry for 25 February 1760 is an estimate for a proposed boat to be built by Henry Holloway Shipwright for the officer of Studland, the length from stem to stern to be 15½ft, with a breadth 5ft 8in and a depth of 22in.

The report states what material would be used to build the boat: the stem, stern post and square of the stern and timbers grown to the work - good oak; the middle blank of the bottom to be deal and the sides of oak and two boards each side the keelson to be built with $^5/_8$in Elm boards, with rudder, tiller, iron work for the same. Other details mentioned:

Two good ringbolts and a pair of oars, with mast.

The cost of the boat fully painted was £5 5*s*

The sails to be provided by William Harrison sailmaker comprising four cloths 15ft deep, £1 5*s*.

Revenue vessels built by John Gely shipbuilders at Cowes:

1795 – *Swan IV* – Cutter - Stationed at Cowes

1795 – *Diligence II* – Cutter

1796 – *Eagle* – Cutter

1797 – *Speedwell III* – Cutter

1798 – *Swan V* – Cutter – Stationed at Cowes

1799 – *Dolphin* – Cutter

1799 – *Falcon* – Cutter

1800 – *Tartar* – Cutter

A famous landmark at the entrance to Christchurch Harbour and built on the sand spit is the Black House. Originally a boat builder's house, this building has been standing there for nearly 200 years. Vessels called Guinea boats were favoured by the smugglers of the time until they became prohibited. The Guinea boats built at Christchurch were unlicensed and their crews took enormous risks during the Napoleonic Wars when they illegally exported bullion in the form of sovereigns in belts worn by the sailors; if the boat ever capsized this meant certain death for the sailors.

John Pilgrem of Christchurch constructed a Marsh Boat in 1788 for John Streeter, the notorious Christchurch smuggler. The vessel is reported to have had a false bottom, ledgers etc. The vessel was 126ft long and cost 2*s* 6*d* per foot to build, a total of £15 4*s*.

Smuggling vessels

The smugglers did not always have the best luck as is shown on 21 November 1783 when a small smuggling cutter ran ashore near the mouth of Poole Harbour and was totally lost; two of the crew were drowned.

The following are more examples but as you can imagine there were many more vessels to choose from:

Ann – sloop – weighing in at 14 tons – seized on 5 June 1805 by Robert Willis carrying fifty-four casks of foreign spirit.

Diana – Smuggling Cutter Poole

Harmayne – from Cherbourg

Hazard – sloop square stern of Rye – weighing in at 14 tons – size 34.4'x10.4'x6' – seized on 1 June 1805 by Robert Willis carrying thirty-three casks of foreign spirit and 400lb of tobacco.

Integrity of Jersey captured by the *Fancy* and brought into the Port of Poole, captured at around 1 a.m. on 9 February 1829 by a boat rowing guard off Studland.

Wallard – Cornish Ranger is belonging to Causand – a Lugger weighing in at 300 tons and armed with 26 guns manned by 60-80 men. A very prolific smuggling vessel; for example, in 1783 on 21 and 30 September landed 3,000 casks of foreign spirits and 10-12 tons of tea brought into the country in convoy with three other luggers, and worked the coast between the Needles and Christchurch Head; working from Guernsey once or twice a fortnight and Dunkerque in France once in three weeks.

The *Civil Usage* – in at 73 tons, a lugsail vessel, clincher built. The size of the vessel was 77ft long and 14ft 2in broad, and armed with twenty 6-pounders. Captain was a Captain May and is believed to be one of the vessels used by the smugglers at the battle of Mudeford in 1784, and seized at the time by George Sarmon commander of the *Swan* revenue cutter.

The *Ranger* – a privateer from Guernsey landed a cargo in 1762 near Poole.

The *Wasp* – weighing in at 270 tons and armed with twenty-two guns manned by sixty to eighty men and worked the coast between the needles and Christchurch Head capable of carrying 3,000 casks of spirits and 8–10 tons of tea; working from Guernsey once or twice a fortnight and Dunkerque in France once in three weeks.

The *Phoenix* – weighing in at 96 tons, a lugsail vessel, clincher built and at the time of the battle of Mudeford was two years old. The size of the vessel was 90ft long and 15ft and armed with twenty-two 6-pounders was owned by John Streeter from Christchurch and captained by a Mr Parrott. It was one of the vessels used by the smugglers at the battle of Mudeford in 1784, and seized at the time by George Sarmon commander of the *Swan* revenue cutter.

The *Vigilant* – a sloop which made a very successful run in 1796, right up Poole Harbour, anchored off the quay at night and unloaded her cargo of tubs of spirits into punts which then went up the shallow waters of Holes Bay.

The types of vessels used by the smugglers and the revenue men varied mainly due to their availability but both would have been clinker built vessels normally single masts, deep keeled fast cutters with long bowsprits capable of about 12 knots. The revenue cutters were limited in their design such that they were only allowed sprits of ⅔ the length of their hulls; no jibs were permitted on the bowsprit which meant that there were no flying jib sails, but jib topsails were permitted.

To help the smugglers in their escape from the custom cutters, in the seventeenth century the design of the smugglers' vessels changed; the old design of the square-rigged was amended to fore and aft design with 3 short masts. This change in the rigging made the vessels faster and much more manoeuvrable; for example, the vessel could beat into an adverse wind and sail off whilst vessels with square riggers would have to wait until the wind changed. As time went by the designs were further modified evolving into shallow draft which allowed the vessels to come closer inshore meaning the smugglers could offload their contraband easier and in some cases even beach the ships ready to float them off again at high tide.

Then there were the open boats, double-ended yawls, lugger rigged, 70ft in length which could carry between 500 and 1,000 casks, and by drawing little water could also be run ashore to be unloaded by gangs of smugglers, which could be sixty to eighty men and in some cases substantially more, on the shore. These vessels, luggers and yawls were designed on the lines of the Old Norse vessels, seaworthy but capable of being run ashore.

The smugglers also used long, narrow, shallow and fast galleys with a removable lug sail 40ft upwards in length with six oars. These could be constructed to take ten to twelve oars by shifting the thwarts, making them very fast. These vessels would be unlicensed and if over 28ft in length were illegal. If these vessels were caught and seized they would be broken up and not sold at public auction along with their cargo. The smugglers liked these vessels as they were low lying and very difficult to see, especially at night. These vessels would be fast and a trip from Cherbourg to Hengistbury Head could be done in one night and speeds of 9.5 knots could be reached.

One of the many rules was the amount boats and the length of the sail boat. A vessel under 70 tons (only exception would be if the vessel was a square-rigged ship or brig) was only allowed one boat and that must not exceed 14ft and vessels between 70 tons and not over 150 tons were only allowed two boats and the largest of the two boats must not be any longer than 15ft, and of course they must not be a smuggler!

Under the law any small unlicensed vessels not engaged in foreign trade and found in the English Channel more than nine miles from the English coast were considered intent on smuggling and were liable to seizure and open for prosecution.

Smuggling vessels could carry up to 400 4/6 gallon casks. In the winter season this fell to between thirty and 100. One-hundred ton vessels could carry 400–800 such casks making up to two trips per week or three in a fortnight. Within one year along the coast from Poole to Christchurch saw 8,000 gallons of spirits and along the Purbecks 40,000 gallons of spirits had been smuggled into the country, a very large amount of lost revenue for the government of the time. The goods would have been moved inland using wagons, carts horses etc. to their waiting customers.

The smugglers would always try to be one step ahead of the revenue men coming up with more and more ingenious hiding places, in fact not much different to the smugglers of today really. Many of the vessels used by the smugglers had hiding places, places that from a quick glance could not be detected easily thus avoiding the duties to be paid. For example, some had false bulkheads, false bottoms and even in one case a second deck 3in above the main deck where the goods could be hidden away from the prying eyes of the customs men, then the smugglers would fit tea cases between the vessels timbers in such away as they resembled part of the vessel. Other examples of how the smugglers would deceive the revenue are impressive: hiding tea under the cape or petticoat trouser that would be worn by the fisherman and pilots and sewing pouches into their garments, waistcoats, and thigh pieces that would be worn by the sailors and passengers; by hiding the tea over their person - a total of 30lb of tea could be smuggled in avoiding the duty. Every part of the ship was a potential hiding place. Wooden fenders would be hollowed out and filled with tobacco, ropes intertwined with the tobacco, even in those days the money that could be made from this illicit trade was worth taking risks. The smugglers also would hide their contraband under other cargo: for example, the *Mary Ann* of Poole entered the harbour in 1835 with 800 tubs hidden under her cargo of coal. Within the same year another vessel the *Emulation* registered at Cowes had a very clever hiding place under her ballast for 108 tubs of spirits and fifty-six flagons of spirits and a small quantity of tea.

The law was soon changed on how the duty was charged on importing tobacco. A manufacturer of tobacco realised a good way to import more tobacco into the country legally was to dry out the tobacco, as moisture adds extra weight to the tobacco. By drying the tobacco in special drying rooms and tightly packing it into barrels, the weight of 100lb of tobacco could be reduced to 60lb. When imported, it would be delivered to the factory where it would be unpacked and open up to the air to allow moisture to rehydrate the tobacco, making a tidy profit for the factory owner. Maybe John Streeter of Christchurch used this method when he imported tobacco into his factory at Stanpit. But this all changed when the duty was paid on the amount of moisture contained therein, and made it less profitable when the duty of dried tobacco was high.

In 1783 at the end of the war between the American-English colonies and Great Britain, ex-privateers were converted into smuggling vessels matching the fire power and this evened the odds between the custom vessels and the smugglers' boats.

To give an idea of the level of the smuggling, customs records show that in 1764 ships of the East India Company smuggled tea into England estimated at £7 million annually.

The smugglers generally preferred to land their cargoes and move them inland as soon as possible but sometimes to avoid being captured and lose their valuable cargo to the revenue men the smugglers would sink their cargo until the coast was clear and they could land the cargo without been detected. This practice known as sinking or 'sowing the crop', was so common that the merchants would supply the tubs ready prepared to be sunk, and the raft of tubs would normally be prepared for sinking before the smugglers reached the English coast, so if discovered by the revenue men then they could cast the raft overboard quickly and with ease, saving the cargo, ready to be collected at later date. Nearly all smuggling vessels would have been fitted with what they used to call a tub rail and this was a wooden rail that ran the length of the vessel and the preparation to sow the crop could even go as far as having tubs already attached to the drift line with all of the sinking stones attached and when passing over the spot where they wanted to sink the cargo they would simple cut the lines to the crop and they would sink down into position ready to be collected at a later date.

The method of attaching the tubs to the drift line was quite simple really: a rope was passed around the tubs twice, one at each end forming a loop in the middle which was attached to the drift line, also creating a handle, which would be used later by the tub men when the tubs were carried away after being landed. The tubs of spirits or tea (packed in waterproof bags before been packed in barrels) would then be attached to a drifting line, approximately forty or fifty tubs at a time with a weight, a large stone known as a sinking stone, between each tub and would be cast overboard. Anchors would then be bent attached to either end stopping the raft from drifting away. The raft of tubs would be floating just below the water level ready to be picked up by the smugglers later. The site would be marked by a cork buoy attached to the raft by the means of a length of string or a lobster line on a known bearing so the tubs could be recovered easily. This process would be carried out whilst the vessel was amongst a fleet of fishermen to aid the hiding of the casks.

A second method of sinking a cargo was to create a pyramid of tubs with the lower ones painted green whilst the upper ones were painted white and attached to the seabed using a grappling iron. The fact they were very low in the water meant that they would be very hard to see, except if you knew where they were.

To recover the tubs would be easy as long as you knew where they were! But revenue men did not know and one of the most unpopular tasks for the revenue men was to go down at dawn along the coast on a winter's day dredging for sunken contraband, spending sixteen hours or so at sea, cold and wet dragging a 'creeping iron' along the seabed in the hope of catching the kegs.

The smugglers would go out knowing where they had hidden the contraband and then the whole raft could be 'crept up' using rakes and grappling irons or many just towed the entire raft ashore under water. Once a shore they would be met by a gang of smugglers who would either load the tubs onto waiting carts or horses; sometimes they would be carried away by tub men who would carry normally two or three tubs at a time one or two strapped to their back and one strapped to the front. The pay for this would be 2/6d per keg. If the cliff was too steep, then a chain of men would be formed and the kegs passed up the cliffs to the waiting transport.

Sinking the cargo did not go without problems though, for example if there was a storm and rough seas it was known for the stones to become detached from the raft and then the tubs would float to the surface, break free and in many cases dashed on the rocks, only to be destroyed, losing the contents to the sea. The site chosen for sinking tubs needed to be chosen carefully; the seabed can hide surprises. Soft silt could mean if the raft was not sunken correctly then the tubs might get buried never to be recovered. To overcome this, the smugglers would tie a plank of wood onto the tubs which would give it that little bit more buoyancy allowing the tubs to float just above the sea bed. Also if the tubs were left too long immersed in the sea due to the recovery being too dangerous then the contents would become unusable and these were known as 'Stinkibus'.

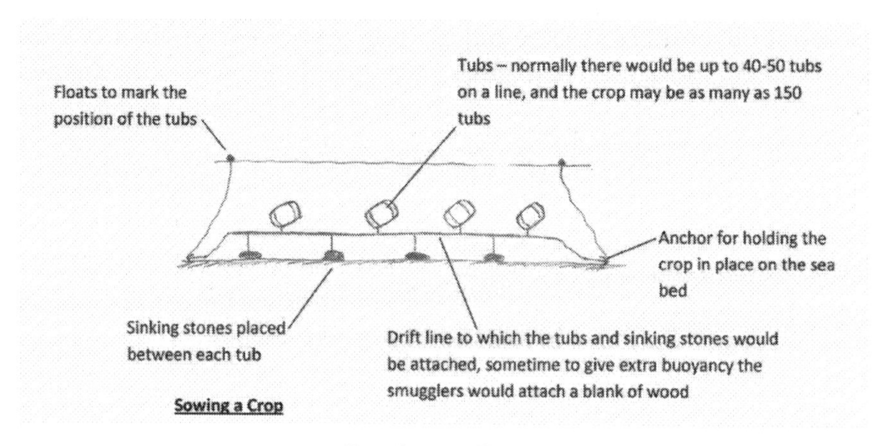

Sowing a Crop

What can go wrong recovering the sunken tubs?

Accidents happen and sunken cargo could just as easy be located and dragged up by fishermen, as happened in November of 1720, 1 mile off shore near Burton Bradstock, but this escalated into a chain of events that ended up with questions being asked in the House of Commons. It also triggered events between the person who had to collect the goods, Philip Taylor, and the Lord of the Manor, Mr Thomas Strangways. The contraband which consisted of twenty-three ankers of brandy and two barrels of wine were brought ashore at Abbotsbury and held by the local excise officer Mr Whitteridge. It was then re-seized by William Bradford the local bailiff to Mr Thomas Stangways (Lord of the Manor) who then stated that this was his master's entitlement to take them for his own use; as Lord of the Manor this was one of his perks. The goods were then kept by Bradford under lock and key. As mentioned earlier Philip Taylor was on a number of occasions requested by a Joseph Hardy (the local customs officer) to re-seize the contraband but to no avail, each time he went to Bradford, a gang of local men would meet him. Soon he realised that he would not succeed and that most of the villagers of Abbotsbury were working for Mr Thomas Stangways. Deciding the only way to seize the contraband would be to enlist the help of the army; he contacted Lt Carr commanding officer of Lord Irwin's Regiment of Horse quartered at Dorchester. On 16 November 1720, the quartermaster William Thomson and Joseph Hardy and eighteen troops set out to William Bradford to re-seize the contraband, and were met by a great angry mob. To try to keep the peace, the local constable was called and Bradford, on seeing the troops, just handed over the keys and Hardy recaptured the kegs of spirits. Unperturbed, Stangways, still not accepting the situation, even claimed the casks were salvage from a wrecked ship, and also made a complaint to why the troops were involved but all to no avail.

Reported in the *Salisbury and Winchester Journal* on 29 February 1824: 'On the 11th inst Mr Martin creeped up off Boscombe, eighty-nine casks of foreign spirits and 1 cask of tea which was seized and placed within his Majesty's warehouse at Poole.'

Mr Martin was once again busy as on 30 July of that year he found and seized ninety-three casks of spirits floating at sea and once again placed them in His Majesty's warehouse at Poole. Obviously a failed attempt at sinking; it is possible that they broke away during a storm.

There are many things that can go wrong whilst trying to recover the sunken contraband; in 1826 when a crew employed on the coastguard off Portland under the orders of Captain Boxer RN made a seizure of thirty-seven casks of spirits, which was only part of the cargo that had been sunk off Church Hope. The smugglers, not wanting to lose their valuable cargo, made a daring attack on the boatman with stones and weapons and it appears that one, William Stephen, was pronounced by the surgeons to be in a very dangerous state. The report suggests that the rescue of the contraband by the smugglers was successful, but the perpetrators were known to Captain Boxer who took the necessary measures to apprehend them.

Whilst landing and retrieving sunken contraband things could go wrong for the smugglers, as in this particular case. Early one morning in Nov 1851 a small cutter rigged vessel sailed around Durlston Head from the west crewed by two. However, they were spotted by the coastguard James Mitchell who was on duty as the day watchman at a spot called Battery. Thinking the vessel to be a smuggling vessel he called the Chief boatman who then hailed the *Gertrude* asking the crew to board the suspected smuggling vessel. Mitchell was also ordered to search and examine the western part of Swanage coastguard station taking with him boatman Walter Proton. He searched the *Five Guard* and finding nothing moved onto the *Sixth Guard* at a place known as Ragged Rock. Looking over the cliff he noticed tubs in the water close to the rocks and attached to a warp (tow rope). Sending Walter off to report the find he noticed a man on the rocks which he recognised as Richard Champ, where upon he called back Walter to change the message. As Richard Champ moved away, a strong smell of spirits reached James Mitchell while under the cliff and then he noticed several broken tubs and tub staves thrown out from the spot where Richard Champ went, some of them falling back into the sea; some had fallen onto the rocks splitting open and spilling their contents. Unfortunately for the men, they were trapped on the rocks until the afternoon when the *Gertrude* was able to get close enough to pick them up.

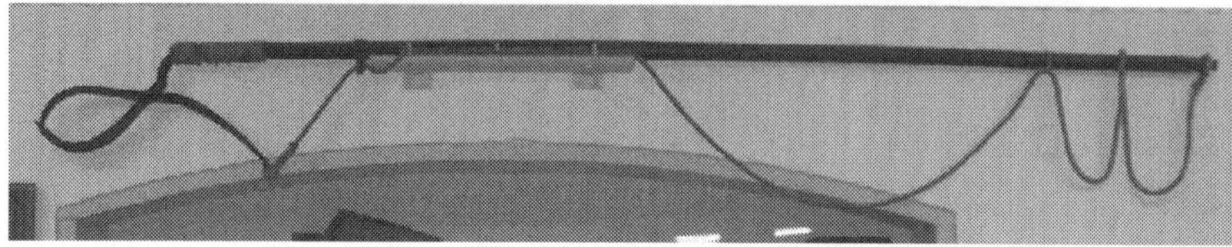

Long pole grappling iron used by the smugglers to recover the kegs

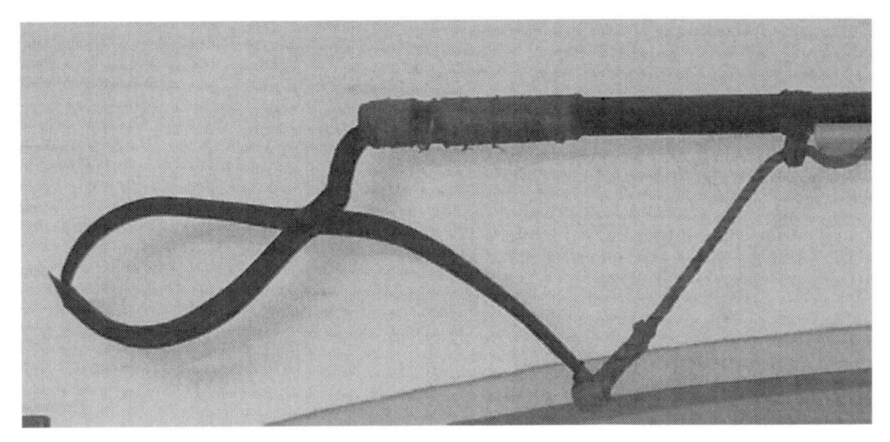

Long pole grappling iron used by the smugglers to recover the kegs

At low tide the *Gertrude* only managed to pick twenty-five broken tubs, some tub staves and the warp or tow rope with thirty tub slings still attached, along with five quarts of spirits in a hollow of a rock which were seized and taken to Poole Custom House.

The two smugglers were identified as Richard and Fredrick Champ, two notorious smugglers from Osmington Mills near Weymouth, and the vessel was the *Grande Famille* of Cherbourg.

The two smugglers were taken to Dorchester Gaol where records show they were fined £100, but served six months in default of payment.

Another one of Mitchell's successes was in 1851 when a crop of tubs was towed into Poole Harbour by a canoe manned by two people. The canoe was intercepted by the coastguard boat and the only reason they realised that something was not quite right was when the oars struck tubs that were about 1ft underwater. Altogether there were about 150, all with a canvas bag of 6lb of sand tied to them, which kept the tubs underwater. Again on 9 June 1852 smugglers managed to land fifteen to twenty tubs at Chapmans Pool only to lose the remaining 101 tubs to the coastguard who 'crept up' the remaining crop.

The last run of smuggled goods in West Dorset occurred in the mid-nineteenth century. The contraband was sunk for six months, moved several times and finally landed at Abbotsbury. The kegs originally came over from France following a fortnight of fog and were dropped on a trawler ground. 120 tubs, half of the crop, were picked up by a ship as it came around the bill from Portland Harbour only to lose one of the tubs. The smugglers attempted to land the kegs at Burton but due to the great surf no landing could be made so they made the kegs into a raft and eventually landed and loaded them into wagons waiting in a potato field. Old Bartlett's gang tried to land the remaining half of the crop east of Seatown, but they were unluckily spotted by preventative men. At day break some tackle was hitched, the boat was put to sea and the tubs went over the side again. Later a Charmouth man helped raise some and landed them at the sluices of Bridport Harbour until once more the landing was seen and the boat ran up the coast to Abbotsbury where the remaining part of the cargo was landed.

As a result of the successful seizure and detecting the landing by Richard and Fredrick Champ, James Mitchell was promoted in February 1852.

Acts against smuggling

To aid the revenue officers in the fight against the smugglers the government started giving them more and more powers, passing many acts of parliament that would allow them to detain, arrest and stop anybody unloading contraband and running the goods inland and to place them in front of the local Justice of the Peace. They would be then transferred to the local gaol without bail until the next general quarterly session. The acts of parliament also started to restrict the movement of the vessels carrying illegal goods used by the smugglers by making it illegal to hover around ports and off the British coast to a distance of 2 leagues and for the vessel to not exceed 200 tons otherwise punishment would be the vessel forfeited and all cargo and ships furniture would be seized by His Majesty's officers. The fate of these vessels could be one of two ways: if they were any use to His Majesty's service then they would be used as they did with the seized vessel *Nancy;* however, if of no use, the hulls would be broken up destroyed or burnt and the cargo and ships furniture would be auctioned off with the proceeds divided up between the officers that seized the vessel and the government.

Vessels carrying the cargoes would have been known to hover for many days off the coast waiting for the smugglers to gather the gangs together and to signal when all was ready to land the cargoes. These acts of hovering were first reported in 1719 with many more following through the years.

There were Acts which determined the size and number of oars permitted as early as 1721. The passing of these acts drove the smugglers to land their cargoes straight away, hiding them in their many hiding places along the coast, which was even more risky, as on the land power was given to the officers to check, detain, stop and arrest a group of two or more people on horseback in a carriage or cart. If they were carrying more than 6lb of tea and more than 5 gallons of spirituous liquor without the proper paperwork or carrying weapons and in disguise, then they also could be arrested and placed before the Justice of the Peace and passed to the local gaol without bail until the next quarterly session.

Another interesting part of the 1779 act even goes into the dealer's affairs. Those that imported tea, coffee, coconuts and chocolate had to display above the door 'Dealer in tea, coffee, coconuts and chocolate' and those that imported brandy and foreign spirits had to display above their doors 'importer or dealer in Foreign Spirits Liquor'. Failure to do so would be met with a fine of £200 for the tea dealer and £50 for the dealer in foreign spirits. As early as 1736 an act was passed that if you dangerously wounded an excise officer the penalty would have been death, and if you in anyway got in the way of him doing his duty or if you resisted arrest then you may have ended up being transported for five years or being whipped and jailed for a month and got a sentence of hard labour. Another part this act was the 'Act of Indemnity'. This clause within the act caused many a battle between the smugglers and the way it worked was that if a smuggler turned on his fellow smugglers and passed on details to the revenue officers he or she would be granted a full pardon. But as already mentioned it was not wise to make enemies of the smugglers and the act was not very successful. The 1736 act was revised in 1781 when things did get even tougher for the smugglers; if two or three people were caught armed with a firearm or an offensive weapon and assembled in the act of exporting, re-landing wool or contraband, or rescuing or taking away the same after seizure by the custom officers and even worse to injure any customs officers whilst they were on duty would be met with a severe penalty and if lawfully convicted of the crime, punishment was death without the benefit of clergy. If the person managed to escape, then their names would be advertised in the London Gazette and they would have forty days to surrender. If they did not their sentence would be death and anybody that assisted them in hiding or assisting them would be transported to the plantations for seven years and to help in the hunt, a reward would have been offered for £500 for any information to apprehend the smugglers.

As a result of a shortage of men to fight the many wars England was involved in the government went soft on the smugglers and after great consultation another act, the Act of Oblivion, in 1782, was passed. This was similar to the act of 1736 except that in this act if the smuggler could find 2 people, one able seaman and one able lands man, who would be willing to take their place then the smugglers would be allowed to go free and released from a previously imposed fine of £500. If the smugglers found 4 people to take his place that would be two able seamen and two able lands men, then he or she would be released from any crime except for the murder of a revenue man. This led to those that could afford to pay people to take their place and even answer adverts to those willing to take their place. One person who may have done this was Isaac Gulliver, a notorious smuggler.

In 1784 Revenue cutters were allowed to fire upon the vessels they were chasing if they did not bring to after been ordered to stop. Under section 23 of the 1784 Act for the Prevention of Smuggling, customs personnel were indemnified against prosecution for any damages or injury they might cause, provided they had hoisted a defaced Blue Ensign Pendant. Section 24 made owners and/or commanders of merchant ships that hoisted the flags of the HM ships or revenue vessels liable to a fine of £500. By 1802 an act was introduced which amended the hovering act to a distance of 8 leagues from the; and also in this act if you were caught lighting fires to signal smugglers' vessels hovering offshore then you would be arrested and fined £100.

By 1816 when the Royal Navy took over the manning of the revenue cutters, an act came out giving them the same powers of stop, detain and arrest and the rewards from the seizure as the revenue officers.

Over the next few years more acts of parliament were introduced: in 1818 more powers were given to the arrest of anybody on board a suspected smuggling vessel that could not prove they were passengers.

If they could not prove it, they would be arrested and taken before the local Justice of the Peace and then onto the local gaol. Within these acts of parliament any persons that were transported to the local gaol awaiting their trial could also have been at any time transported and impressed into the navy, but the government of the time realised some of the problems and started to make things easier for them by ensuring in an act of 1830 that the families and wives of all smugglers impressed into the navy should be looked after; that half of all wages should be made available to support their wives and families, also after their term of five years of impressments that they should be allowed to leave the ship and come home. Finally, the act that finished smuggling as they knew it at that time was the act of 1848. The Corn Act removed duty on many of the items smuggled into the country virtually killing the trade-off overnight.

All the acts of parliament against the smugglers did not have the effect that was required; yes, it did reduce smuggling but did not stop it. The only real effect was that the smugglers did not want to face the penalties gradually being put in place by these acts. As the years passed the penalties got more and more severe, so the smugglers would just abandon the cargo rather than be caught with the evidence. For example, before the act against a ship hovering off the coast was passed the smugglers would wait until they could land the cargo safely and the revenue men were not to be seen. Then after 1719 when the first of the hovering acts came into place the smugglers would make quick fast landings and then have to hide all the contraband along the coast in the caves, undergrowth etc. where it would be discovered fairly easily by the revenue men. If a ship was being chased by the revenue cutters, then once again the smugglers would prefer to sacrifice the cargo rather than lose their ship and freedom or even worse scenario been impressed in the navy.

The penalty in many cases for crimes of smuggling was death by hanging, but reading through the Dorchester Gaol records all death sentences passed were never carried out. The prisoners either stayed in prison or were impressed into His Majesty's Navy. However, there are cases of smugglers being hanged for murder, as mentioned in this book, but they were for serious crimes against the revenue services.

Appendix

Some of the custom officers stationed at Poole, Weymouth and in surrounding areas

Poole Customs			
Collectors		Wareham	
Thomas Miller		John Florence	1758 Died 1777
William Milner	1758 - Dismissed	Nathaniel Florence	1777
John Hudden	1758 - resigned in 1778		
John Lander	1778 - deceased 1806	Christchurch	
William Wilson	1806	Abraham Pike	
David Lander	1807	Buffey	1759
Deputy Comptrollers		Hookey	1759
Mr Smith	1772	Newsam Bursey	1762
Samuel Weston	1758	Francis Stokes	1762
John Bowles	1758–1772	John Reeks	1762
Samuel Weston	1772–1785	Mr Bacon	1803

Robert Weston	1785	Mr Preston	1803
Edward Allen	1792	Mr Jones	1803
		John Bursey	
		Lymington	
Custom Surveyors		Mr Pritchard	
Thomas Barney	1682 – Removed from duty; suspended		
Thomas Wise	1761 – Died 1763	Supervisors of Excise	
John Hide	1764	Thomas Ireland (Wimborne)	1759
Peter Joliff	1774	John Pring	1773 (Christchurch)
John Strong	1795	Robert Shutt	1778
Excise Officer		Land Waiter and Deputy Searcher	
Mr Burgess (Ringwood)		Joseph Skutt	1761 Died 1766
Mr Weakly (Wimborne)		William Pike	1766
Mr Wood	1763		
Tidesman and Boatman		Land Waiter and Deputy Searcher	

Joseph Rowe (Studland)	1759	Waiters and Searchers		
Peter Shanks	1760		Poole	
Robert Thombs	1760		David Durell	1778 Died 1774
George Olive	1760 – Drowned on duty 1760		Thomas Tite	1766
Stephen Morris	1761		Joseph Wadham	1766
Cartridge	1763		Warren Lisle	
John Mercer	1818			
John Rigler	1818		Wareham	
Tidewaiters			Richard Cole	1770 Died 1774
William Vincent			Henry Best Land	1774
Thomas Keeping			Nathaniel Florance	1777
Richard Checkford			Coast Waiter	
Weigher			James Seager	1758
Thomas Howell			Boatman at Brownsea under Captain Wadham	
Supervisor of Riding Officers			Peter Phippard	
Christchurch			Joseph Barnes	

Joshua Stephens Jeans	1759	Timothy Stevens	
Robert Reeks	1793	John Arrowsmith (Commander of boat at Brownsea Island)	
Riding Officers		Studland	
Poole		George Bayly	
Thomas Cload	1758	Mr Snook	
Robert Cleeves	1758 Died 1760	Salt Officer	
Joseph Olive	1760	Mr Tibbs (Parkstone)	
John Coombs	1760	Sitter at Swanage	
William Belcher	1770	Joseph Carter	
Martin Wightwick	1774		
Kimmeridge			
John Wise Junior	1785		
Thomas Coombs	1770		

Mr Tewkesberry			
Weymouth Customs			
Collectors		Osmington	
Jackson	1699	George Mortimer	1733
Southwick	1700	William Hobbs	1735
Thomas Bower	1700 -1716	William Stokesley	1743 – 1747
Robert Watts	1716 -1729	John Theddam	1747
William Stammers	1736 – 1739 - Dissmised	Henry Weston	1748
Edward Tizard Junior	1739 - 1741	Edward Thorne	1754
Richard Arbuthnot	1741	Abbotsbury	
Richard Jordan	1742 - 1747	Edward Thorne	1740
John Russell	1748 - 1759	George Limbury	1754
Joseph Swaffield	1759 – 1770	Benjamin Hounsell	Died August 1719
William Weston	1770	William M Taunton	
		Joshua Beach	

Philip Taylor	1716-1720	Lagnton	
		William Smirke	1733
Deputy Comptrollers		Edward Bayley	1741 – 1750
Watson	1699	John Noise	1750
George Beck Junior	1700–1717	Wyke	
Stephen Harvey	1730–1749 becoming the collector at Exeter	Henry Weston	1754
Robert Poulden	1749	Chirckerill	
Collectors Clerk		John Noise	1763
John Crouch	1738	Coastguard Boatman–Swanage	
Supervisor of Riding Officers		James Mitchell	1839
Robert Henley	1735–1743	Walter Prouten	
Warren Lisle			
Surveyor		Comissioned Boatman–Swanage	
George Beck	1717	James Mitchell	1845
Searcher			
Warren Lisle			
Land Surveyors		William Biles	
Samuel	1735–1756	Warren Lisle	

Templeman			
Tide Surveyors		Thomas Packer	
Jonathan Cook	1714–1717	Samuel Templeman	
John Swanton	1719		
Thomas Bishop Senior	1742 Superannuated	Riding Officer – Ringwood	
Thomas Bishop Junior	1742–1770 Drowned on duty	Mr Critchell	
Robert Penny	1770		
John Bishop	Drowned 25 April 1770		
Tidesman and Boatman			
Barker Russell	1742		
Thomas Dyer	1742		
John Loder			
Henry Young			
William Randall			

Phillip Allan			
James Dyer			
William M Taunton			
John Hickman	Drowned 25 April 1770		
Thomas Andrew	Drowned 25 April 1770		
John Pearce	Drowned 25 April 1770		
Robert Johnson	Drowned 25 April 1770		
Tidewaiters			
Thomas Summers			
Extra Tidesman and Boatman and Coal Meter			
Thomas Bagg	Drowned 25 April 1770		
Land Waiter			
Thomas Ledoze	1712		
Riding officers			
Portland			
Edward	1730		

Tizard			
William Smirke	1733		
George Limbury	1747		
John Noise	1757		
Dorchester			
John Oldfield	1712–1761		
William Old	1761		

A Smuggler's Dictionary

Anker – Cask generally holding about 8½ gallons of spirits. Sizes varied from 6½ to 9 gallons
Half-Anker – Cask holding approximately 4½ gallons and weighed approximately 56lb
Barton – An archaic English word meaning lands of the manor or meadow
Barrel – 36 gallons
Barque – A barque, barc, or bark is a type of sailing vessel with three or more masts, which are square-rigged
Barquentine – A barquentine (also spelled barkentine, or in Italian *bergantina*) is a sailing vessel with three or more masts: they feature a square-rigged foremast and fore and aft rigged main, mizzen and all other masts
Bat – A weapon used by smugglers to protect themselves from the revenue men, consisting of a pole approximately 6ft long and usually made of ash
Batman – A smuggler armed with a bat to defend themselves from the revenue men.
Bill of Lading – Document issued by a carrier to a shipper acknowledging receipt of a cargo on board and for conveyance to a named place of delivery. Term derives from the verb 'to lade' meaning to load a cargo onto ship or some form of transport.
Boatman – One who works on, deals with or operates boats
Bow Street Runners – The Bow Street Runners were established in 1749 by the author Henry Fielding and have been referred to as London's first police force. They started out as just six members. The group was disbanded in 1839
Bohea Tea – An inferior quality of black tea grown late in the season
Book of Rates – The official book listing the duties payable on imports/exports
Boskom – The old name for Boscombe (near Bournemouth)
Carbine – A short firearm
Caterpillar – A wool smuggler
Carvel-built vessel – In boat building, carvel built or carvel planking is a method of constructing wooden boats and tall ships by fixing planks to a frame so that the planks butt up against each other, edge to edge, gaining support from the frame and forming a smooth hull.

Such planking requires caulking between the joints over and above that needed by the clinker-built technology, but gives a stronger hull capable of taking a variety of full-rigged sail plans. Carvel built construction enables greater length and breadth of hull as well as superior sail rigs because of its stronger framing

Centum – The hundredweight or centum weight (abbreviated cwt.) is a unit of weight defined in pounds. Its British definition is not the same as that used in North America. The two are distinguished by speaking of the long-hundredweight: 112lb versus the short-hundredweight: 100lb

C.F.M. – Civilian First Mate

C.S.M. – Civilian Second Mate

C.C. – Civilian Commander

D.O. – Deputed Officer

Clinker-built vessel – Clinker building is a method of constructing hulls of boats and ships by fixing wooden planks and, in the early nineteenth century, iron plates to each other so that the planks overlap along their edges. The overlapping joint is called a land. The technique was developed in northern Europe and successfully used by the Vikings

Coastguard – The service was introduced in 1822 mainly to combat smuggling

Coast Waiter – An officer who witnesses the landing of goods moved from one part of the country to the next

Cockets – Receipts of payment of duty, which would have been recorded in the Port Book

Collector of custom – The chief officer in a port; they recorded details of the imports/exports and successful seizures. Also oversaw of all other officers

Composition – A fine for smuggling, calculated according to value of goods seized and the smuggler's means

Comptroller – Answered to the Collector of Customs and oversaw the accounts put together by the Collector of Customs and sent copies to the Comptroller General

Condemned – When contraband or vessels are seized and passed to the Crown. Illicit goods would be sold and seized, vessels may be sold or used by officers of customs e.g. *Nancy*

Customs Waiter – Responsible for surveying of coast wise trading

Creeping – Fishing for sunken kegs of spirits or contraband that have

been thrown overboard and sunk in the form of a raft, held down with rocks. Ready to be collected at a later date
Creeping Irons – Grappling irons or hooks used to recover sunken casks.
Crop – Cargo of contraband
Crown – 5*s*
Customer – Customs officer originally appointed to send a copy of the collector's accounts to the treasury. By 1782 role was considered obsolete and sinecure office which 'ought' to be abolished
Custom Duty – Import/Export tax
Cutter – A small single-masted vessel, fore and aft rigged, with two or more headsails, often a bowsprit, and a mast set farther back than a sloop
Darks – Moonless night; best time to go smuggling
Debentures – Certificate of refund of duty due on imported goods to be exported
Discontinuance – Used in the context of paying off a custom vessel e.g. *Nancy* in 1798
Donkey – Single legged stool used by coastguards, forerunner of the shooting stick
Dowlas – A coarse linen or cotton cloth
Dragger Boats – Small boats usually used for getting oysters up from the seabed
Dragoon – Mounted soldier, armed with carbine and sword
Drawback – Refund of Excise duty
Dry Goods – Non-liquid contraband, especially tea
Duffer – Unmounted contraband carrier who would carry up to 1 cwt. of tea or tobacco hidden in the lining of his coat
Excise Duty – Tax on goods produced and sold within the country
Extraman – Tidewaiter or boatman hired on a casual basis
Firkin – 9 gallons (English)
Flasker – Smuggler of liquor
Flint – Smuggler's warning light
Free Trader – Name of a smuggler
Freighter – Person responsible for buying contraband abroad
Flotsam – Cargo that is lost off a vessel whilst at sea. Once at sea it is the responsibility of the Admiralty
Galley – Large open boat propelled by oars and sometimes with sails
Gauger – Revenue officer who measured or gauged barrels and other containers

Geneva – Term for gin
Gibbetted – Cage-like structure from which the dead bodies of executed criminals were hanged on public display to deter other existing or potential criminals. To gibbet a criminal is to display the criminal on a gibbet. This practice is also called 'hanging in chains'
Glutman – Extraman
Gobbler – Smuggler's name for a revenue official
Groat – A silver coin, originally 4*d.* piece of Edward I issued from 1279–1662
Guinea boats – In Napoleonic War used to carry sovereigns in belts; certain death if the boat capsized
Hagboat – Type of eighteenth-century merchant vessel with a beak head and hull planking which continued around the stern
Half-Anker – Cask containing about 4 gallons. Used mostly by smugglers in later generations
Hide – Concealing the contraband
Higgling Cart – Cart of a hawker or peddler of small merchandise
Hollands – Dutch gin
Hot – Mixture of gin and beer served warm, a favourite drink of the smugglers
Hoy – A vessel, usually sloop rigged or a heavy barge displacing approximately 60 tons. Word derives from the Middle Dutch Hoey
Hogs Head – A cask containing about 54 gallons of wine/spirits
Hyson Tea – Green tea from China
Iver – The old name for Iford near Christchurch
Jerquer – Another name for a searcher
Jetsam – Cargo that is jettisoned to lighten the vessel. Once at sea it is the responsibility of the Admiralty
Keg – Term for cask
Ketch – A dual-masted fore and aft rigged sailing vessel with a mizzenmast aft of a taller mainmast but forward of the rudder
Kiderkin – 18 gallons
Kingston – An old name for Kinson, a suburb of Bournemouth
Lading – The action of loading shipment, cargo, or freight
Lander – A person who would organise the unloading and rapid removal of the contraband from the coast or landing place
Land Guard – Collective name for customs riding officers
Land sharks – Smugglers name for land-based revenue officers
Land Surveyor – Customs officer in charge of land waiters

Land Waiter – Customs officers responsible for recording quantity and quality of all imported goods on landing
League – Nautical term for a distance at sea no longer used today. Equates to 3 miles or 4.8km
Lugger – Two or three-mast vessel with four cornered sail set fore and aft
October – The strongest beer brewed in the month of October
Offing – Nautical term- it is the part of the sea that cannot be seen from land, excluding those parts that are near the shore.
Owler – Wool smugglers were known as Owlers because the wool was smuggled at night
Militia – Non-professional military force, employed as and when needed
Noyau – French Liqueur
Packet – Vessel that carried passengers and mail
Philistines – What the smugglers use to call revenue men
Pipes of wine – Wine cask containing about 105 gallons of wine
Port of Staple – Ports that were only allowed to land and export wool
Porter – Contraband carrier
Privateer – Privately owned vessels, armed and licensed by the government to capture enemy vessels
Rhenish – Wine from the Rhine valley
Riding Officers – Mounted custom officers
Rummage – To search for contraband
Run – A smuggling operation; movement of contraband inland from the coast
Schooner – Sailing vessel characterised by the use of fore and aft sails on two or more masts with the forward mast being no taller than the rear masts. Schooners were first used by the Dutch in the sixteenth or seventeenth century, and further developed in North America from the early eighteenth century
Scorage – Name given to damage and loss of contraband in transit
Searcher – Worked with the land and customs waiter who examined the ships and goods looking for contraband
Sitter – Coxswain of the vessel
Sloop – Single-masted fore and aft rigged vessel
Smack – An English/American sailing vessel used to bring fish to market. Originally they were cutter rigged but by 1865 the smacks had become so big that the cutter main booms were unusable
Smooch – Mixture of tea, mouldy leaves and sheep dung

Smot Me – To be stabbed in the face by a knife
Soose – Coin
Soosey – A type of cloth
Souchong Tea – A form of black tea originally from the Fujian province in China
Sowing the Crop – When contraband was thrown overboard and sunk ready for collection at a later stage
Spotsman – Member of the smugglers crew responsible for choosing safest landing place
Spout Lantern – A signalling lantern used to send out a beam of light through a long spout attachment
Staples Port – where goods could be imported and exported and a Customs House would be found
Stinkibus – Contaminated tubs – ones that have leaked/polluted after been thrown overboard and been submerged for long periods of time.
Strongwaters – Diluted Brandy
Supervisor of Excise – An officer in charge of Excise Officers in a particular area
Supervisor of riding officers – An officer in charge of several riding officers
Surveyor – Supervising officer of a customs district
Swingels – Swinging part of a flail which falls to the grain when thrashing. Also used as a weapon against the revenue men
Tide Surveyor – Supervisor for tidewaiters. Each would have had a boat with a sitter (coxswain) and six boatmen
Tidesman – Kept watch on-board ship whilst vessel was being unloaded
Tidewaiter – Customs Officer responsible for searching ships arriving into port to ensure that no goods were concealed as contraband
Tierce – provision cask equalling one-third of a pipe
Tub – Small casks
Tub boat – A boat for smuggling small casks
Tubman – A smuggler employed to carry small casks
Turned off – Terminology for being hanged
Vizard – A mask that covered the whole face
Venturer – Somebody who backs a venture financially, in this case smuggling
Warp – Heavy rope or tow rope used when casting tubs overboard

Waterguard – The name for custom officers that worked/operated at sea until 1972. The service was then abolished and the duties passed to HM Customs and Excise
Weigher – Weighed all goods as they were unloaded from the vessels
Working the crop – The art of recovering sunken contraband
Ullaged Cask – Casks that are only partly full
Yawl – Similar to a ketch but with a smaller jigger or mizzenmast stepped abaft the rudder
Yeomanry – Volunteer cavalry force

Etymology of the word smuggle:

The word may have come from the common Germanic verb *smeugan* (Old Norse *smjúga*) meaning 'to creep into a hole'. Alternatively, it may come from the Middle Dutch verb *smokkelen.* There is another version that suggests it may have come from Scandinavian languages: the Danish word *smugle* means 'smuggle' and the Swedish word *smuga* when translated means 'a lurking hole'. There is also the Anglo-Saxon *smugan*, meaning 'to creep', which may be derived from the Icelandic prefix 'smug' which in turn comes from the word *smjuga* and also means 'to creep' or 'creep through a hole'. One can see that there is a common link in the Scandinavian languages.

Smuggler's Timeline:

1275 King Edward I, seeking new revenue, introduced a tax on wool exports of ½ mark (6*s* 8*d* per bag)
1298 Duty due on wool found to be successful so tax was increased on each 364lb bale exported
1337 Temporary ban on wool tax levelled to protect local clothing industry
1353 Certain ports designated as 'Staples' – wool weighed for taxation on King's Beam scales
1452 William Lowe seizes a coastal ship packed with wool and leather
1453 Port of Poole designated Port of 'Staples'
1565 Tobacco introduced into the United Kingdom
1576 Riot at Lyme Regis – a senior official from London dared to search ships for smuggled bullion
1590 Tax introduced on tobacco

1604 New book of rates introduced, list expanded and increased duty on most taxed commodities
1643 Excise tax introduced, to help fund the Civil War, on beer, cider etc. (still in place to this day)
1660 Ban on exporting wool once again in effort to protect English manufacturers being undercut by cheaper foreign labour
1671 Board of customs set up and custom commissioners appointed by the crown
1680 Special ships known as cutters entered into the service of catching smugglers
1683 Excise commissioners introduced – until the excise was formed
1698 Customs commissioners set a fleet of sloops to be a waterguard
1699 Riding Officers – mounted custom officers first appointed
1700 Fourteen revenue cutters on patrol along the coast
1719 Hovering Act introduced
1721 Number of oars in an unlicensed galley restricted to six
1735 Hawkhurst Gang first mentioned
1736 Smuggling act – result of report by Sir John Cope. The Act of Indemnity: any smuggler who admitted to being involved in smuggling before 27 April 1736 was to be pardoned
1740 Revenue officer Thomas Careswell murdered by the Hawkhurst Gang
1746 Duke of Richmond's Act
1748 Leader of the Hawkhurst Gang, Arthur Grey, hanged for the murder of Thomas Careswell
1765 Robert Trotman killed on local beach by excise men
1765 Start of the American Revolutionary War
1761 Crown resumes collection of customs; start of modern customs
1779 Customs officials' uniform introduced
1780 Custom commissioners decide to pay disability pension for injured men in service
1782 The Act of Oblivion – amnesty for smugglers. The Act of Oblivion was similar to the act of 1736 but in this case the smugglers had to find two people who were willing to take their place. If a smuggler found four people to take his place, then they were released from any crime except for the murder of a revenue man
1783 Peace with France (allowing naval ships to assist the custom service)
1783 End of the American Revolutionary War
1784 Battle of Mudeford

1784 Smuggling tea becomes unprofitable – Tax reduced by 119 per cent to 12½ per cent
1788 Captain Warren Lisle – one of the finest customs officers of the time dies at the age of ninety-three
1792 Work started on Christchurch barracks
1809 Introduction of the new force: Preventive waterguard
1815 End of the Napoleonic War
1816 British Navy made responsible for the manning of the revenue cutters
1817 The start of the blockade of the English Channel
1822 Introduction of coastguard service, initially introduced to stop smuggling
1831 Coastguard fully set up
1848 Corn Law Acts – 450 dutiable items removed from the statue book
1909 Custom and Excise combined
1972 Introduction of VAT and decimalisation
1972 Taxation duties taken over by HM Customs and Excise

Common Smuggled Goods

Goods smuggled between 1700 and 1850 along the South of England included:

Spirits – Brandy, Gin, Rum.
Playing Cards.
Foreign Paper.
Logwood.
Wine.
Tobacco/Tobacco stakes.
Tea.
Coffee.
Cocoa Beans.
Cloth.
Silks.
Perfumes.
Figs.
Currants.
Raisins.
Salt from Guernsey/Jersey.
Pepper.
Vinegar.
British Sovereigns (gold coins).

Bibliography & Other Sources

Angel, M.V., *In Search of Isaac Gulliver: Legendary Dorset Smuggler* (2008)
Guttridge, R., *Dorset Smugglers* (1983)
Guttridge, R., *Evening Echo Book of Heritage* (1991)
Hathaway, E., *Smuggler: John Rattenbury and his Adventures in Devon, Dorset and Cornwall 1778–1844* (1944)
Hodges, M.A., *The Smuggler – No Gentleman: Smuggling with Violence around Christchurch and Poole Bays* (1999)
Legg, R., Collier, M. & Perrott, T., *Ghosts of Dorset, Devon and Somerset* (1974)
Miller, A.J., *Baccy, Rum and Tea from Poole* (1979)
Morley, G., *Smuggling in Hampshire and Dorset 1700–1850* (1983)
Powell, M., *The Battle of Mudeford 1784*
Ross, Simpson, I., *The Life of Adam Smith* (2010)
Short, B.C., *Smuggling in Poole, Bournemouth and Neighbourhood* (1927)
Short, B.C., *Smugglers of Poole and Dorset* (1970)
White, A., *18th Century Smuggling In Christchurch* (1973)

Other sources

Bournemouth Evening Echo
The *Hampshire Telegraph*
Poole Letter Book and Articles from the *Salisbury and Winchester Journal*
Dorset History Centre (Dorchester)
Cowes, Poole and Weymouth Letter Book
Inspection reports on Dorchester Prison
Dorchester Prison Records
Dorset: The County Magazine:
No. 1, 1968 'Landing the Kegs', by Ross Brown
No. 2, 1968 'Isaac Gulliver: The Hottest Thief', by V.J Adams
No. 3, 1968
No. 8, 1969
No. 11, 1970
No. 12, 1970
No. 13, 1970
No. 36, 1974
Poole Borough Archives
Red House Museum (Christchurch)
The Records of Riding Officer 1803–1804

Websites

www.osmington.info